THE LLC SECRETS

(LIMITED LIABILITY COMPANY)

How to Start, Run, and Maintain Your Small Business S-Corp and Save on Real Estate, Accounting, and Taxes with The Complete Coursebook on Entrepreneurship.

RICHARD N. WILLIAMS

All right reserved. No part of this publication may be reproduced, distributed or transmitted in any form or by any means including photocopy, recording or other electronic or mechanical methods, without the prior written permission of the publisher, except in the case of brief quotations embodied in critical reviews and certain other noncommercial uses permitted by copyright law.
Copyright Richard N. Williams

TABLE OF CONTENTS

- LLC (LIMITED LIABILITY COMPANY) ... 3
- CHAPTER 1 DEFINITION AND PURPOSE ... 3
- °Advantages and Disadvantages ... 3
- °Comparison with Other Business Structures Formation of an LLC . 3
- CHAPTER 2 STEPS TO FORMING AN LLC ... 3
- °Choosing a Name and Registered Agent ... 3
- °Articles of Organization ... 3
- °Legal and Regulatory Considerations ... 3
- CHAPTER 3 OPERATING AGREEMENT ... 3
- °State Regulation ... 3
- °Compliance Requirements ... 3
- °Tax Implications for LLCs ... 3
- CHAPTER 4 ... 3
- TAX CLASSIFICATION OPTIONS ... 3
- °Pass-through Taxation ... 3
- °Tax Deductions and Credits for LLCs ... 3
- °Accounting Practices for LLCs ... 3
- CHAPTER 5 BOOKKEEPING BASICS ... 3
- °Financial Statements ... 3
- °Tax Reporting and Filing ... 3
- °Real Estate Investing with an LLC ... 3
- CHAPTER 6 ADVANTAGES OF USING AN LLC FOR REAL ESTATE ... 3
- °Purchasing Property through an LLC ... 3
- °Managing Real Estate Investments ... 3
- °Protecting Assets and Liabilities ... 3
- CHAPTER 7 LIMITED LIABILITY PROTECTION ... 3
- °Insurance Considerations ... 3
- °Asset Protection Strategies ... 3
- °Dissolution and Exit Strategies ... 3
- CHAPTER 8 REASONS FOR DISSOLUTION ... 3
- °Winding Up Business Affairs ... 3
- °Closing an LLC ... 3

- °Case Studies and Examples 3
- CHAPTER 9 SUCCESSFUL LLC VENTURES 3
- °Lessons Learned from Failed Ventures 3
- °Future Trends and Considerations 3
- CHAPTER 10 EVOLVING REGULATIONS AND LAWS 3
- °Technological Innovations in LLC Management 3
- °Globalization and International LLCs 3
- CONCLUSION 3
- On LLC (Limited Liability Company) 3
- INTRODUCTION 1

INTRODUCTION TO LLC (LIMITED LIABILITY COMPANY)

In the city of Oklahoma, amidst the towering skyscrapers and bustling streets, there existed a modest yet ambitious LLC (Limited Liability Company) named "Prosperity Ventures." Founded by a group of passionate entrepreneurs, it began as a humble startup with grand aspirations. Their journey wasn't one of fairy tales but rather a testament to resilience, innovation, and the human spirit.

The founders, Emily, David, and Marcus, each brought their unique expertise to the table. Emily, a visionary with a knack for spotting emerging market trends, spearheaded the company's strategic direction. David, a meticulous accountant, ensured financial stability and compliance with tax regulations. Marcus, a seasoned real estate investor, leveraged his network and experience to identify lucrative opportunities for growth.

Their journey began with a modest office space in a rundown building on the outskirts of town. With limited resources but boundless determination, they transformed the space into a vibrant hub of creativity and collaboration. The walls echoed with the sound of brainstorming sessions and the clatter of keyboards as they worked tirelessly to turn their dreams into reality.

As they navigated the complexities of small business formation, taxes, accounting, and real estate, they encountered numerous challenges along the way. From navigating the labyrinth of legal paperwork to weathering economic downturns, the road to success was fraught with obstacles. Yet, with each setback, they emerged stronger and more determined than ever before.

One particularly challenging obstacle came in the form of a looming tax audit. Despite their best efforts to maintain meticulous records and adhere to regulations, they found themselves under scrutiny by the IRS. Faced with the prospect of hefty fines and potential legal repercussions, they refused to back down. Instead, they rallied together, pouring over every document and transaction with a fine-tooth comb. Through sheer determination and unwavering integrity, they emerged from the audit unscathed, their resolve only strengthened by the experience.

Their resilience and innovative spirit didn't go unnoticed. Word of their success spread like wildfire, attracting the attention of investors and potential clients alike. Before long, Prosperity Ventures had outgrown its humble beginnings and expanded into a thriving enterprise with offices across the country.

But amidst their rapid growth and success, they never lost sight of their core values. They remained committed to giving back to their community, supporting local charities, and mentoring aspiring entrepreneurs. Theirs wasn't just a story of financial success but one of human connection and empathy.

One particularly poignant moment came when they stumbled upon an abandoned warehouse in a run-down neighborhood. While others saw blight and decay, they saw potential and opportunity. With their trademark optimism and ingenuity, they transformed the space into a vibrant co-working hub, providing affordable office space and resources to aspiring entrepreneurs from underserved communities.

Their impact reverberated far beyond the confines of their own company, inspiring countless others to pursue their dreams with passion and perseverance. They became beacons of hope in a world too often plagued by cynicism and despair.

As they looked back on their journey, they realized that their success wasn't measured solely in dollars and cents but in the lives they had touched and the legacy they had created. Theirs was a story of triumph against the odds, a testament to the transformative power of resilience, innovation, and the human spirit.

And so, as the sun set on another day in the bustling city, the founders of Prosperity Ventures stood together, their hearts full and their spirits soaring. For they knew that no matter what challenges lay ahead, they would face them head-on, united in their unwavering belief that anything was possible with passion, perseverance, and a dash of ingenuity.

CHAPTER 1
DEFINITION

AND PURPOSE

Restricted Risk Organizations (LLCs) have turned into a famous business structure for business visionaries and entrepreneurs because of their adaptability and security of individual resources. Understanding the definition and reason for LLCs is fundamental for anybody thinking about beginning a business or rebuilding a current one. In this article, we will dig into the complexities of LLCs, investigating their definition, reason, benefits, and drawbacks.

Definition A Restricted Risk Organization (LLC) is a legitimate business structure that joins components of associations and enterprises. It offers restricted responsibility insurance to its proprietors, known as individuals, meaning their own resources are protected from business liabilities. LLCs are represented by state regulations, and their development normally includes recording articles of association with the fitting state organization and drafting a working arrangement that frames the organization's administration structure and functional systems. One of the vital attributes of LLCs is their adaptability regarding the executives and tax assessment. Not at all like partnerships, which have an inflexible progressive construction with investors, chiefs, and officials, LLCs can be overseen by their individuals or assigned directors.

Moreover, LLCs have the choice to pick how they are burdened, either as a pass-through substance like an organization or as a company.

Purpose the main role of shaping an LLC is to restrict the individual obligation of its proprietors while giving an adaptable and charge proficient business structure. How about we investigate the reasons for LLCs in more detail:

Restricted Responsibility Security: The main benefit of an LLC is the insurance it offers to its individuals' very own resources. In case of claims, obligations, or different liabilities brought about by the business, the individuals' very own resources like homes, vehicles, and financial balances are for the most part not in danger. This impediment of obligation gives true serenity to business visionaries and financial backers, permitting them to face challenges without taking a chance with their own monetary security.

Adaptability: LLCs offer a serious level of adaptability as far as the executives' construction, proprietorship, and functional methods. Not at all like enterprises, which have severe necessities for administration and navigation, LLCs can be overseen casually by their individuals or delegated supervisors. This adaptability permits LLCs to adjust rapidly to changing business needs and economic situations.

Go through Tax collection: Of course, LLCs are treated as pass-through substances for charge purposes, implying that the organization's benefits and misfortunes are passed through to the singular individuals and written about in their own assessment forms. This tax collection structure keeps away from the twofold tax assessment that organizations frequently face, where benefits are charged at both the corporate and individual level. Nonetheless, LLCs additionally have the choice to choose corporate tax assessment assuming it adjusts better to their monetary objectives and conditions.

Believability and Incredible skill: Shaping a LLC can improve the validity and amazing skill of a business, particularly while managing clients, clients, and providers. Having "LLC" in the organization name connotes to partners that the business is a legitimately perceived substance with restricted risk security, which can impart certainty and confidence in the brand.

Progression Arranging: LLCs offer more noteworthy adaptability in progression arranging contrasted with sole ownerships and organizations. In case of the passing, handicap, or retirement of a part, the LLC's working understanding can frame strategies for moving proprietorship interests, guaranteeing congruency of the business without disturbance.

Resource Insurance: For people with critical individual resources, like land possessions or venture portfolios, shaping an LLC can give an extra layer of resource security. By holding these resources inside an LLC, proprietors can safeguard them from likely claims or lenders looking to hold onto resources to fulfill obligations. Regardless of these benefits, LLCs additionally have a few limits and downsides that ought to be thought of:

Cost and Intricacy: Setting up and keeping an LLC includes different lawful and authoritative necessities, including recording expenses, yearly reports, and consistency with state guidelines. While the interaction is by and large less complicated and costly than framing a company, it actually requires cautious thought and arranging.

Independent work Assessments: Despite the fact that LLCs offer pass-through tax collection, individuals are commonly dependent upon independent work charges on their portion of the organization's benefits. This extra taxation rate can decrease the duty benefits of working as an LLC, particularly for major league salary workers.

Restricted Life expectancy: In certain states, LLCs have a restricted life expectancy and may break down upon the passing, withdrawal, or liquidation of a part except if the working understanding determines in any case. This absence of unending presence can confound long haul business arranging and coherence.

State-Explicit Guidelines: LLCs are liable to state regulations and guidelines, which can shift essentially starting with one purview then onto the next. This state-explicit guideline might affect the arrangement interaction, administration construction, and expense treatment of LLCs, requiring cautious thought of the pertinent regulations and necessities.

Restricted Obligation Organizations (LLCs) offer business visionaries and entrepreneurs an adaptable and defensive business structure that joins the advantages of restricted risk security with tax collection and functional adaptability. Understanding the definition and motivation behind LLCs is pivotal for coming to informed conclusions about business arrangement and organizing. While LLCs enjoy various benefits, they additionally have limits and contemplations that ought to be weighed cautiously in counsel with lawful and monetary guides. Eventually, the decision to frame an LLC ought to line up with the special requirements, objectives, and conditions of the business and its proprietors.

°Advantages and Disadvantages

Restricted Obligation Organizations (LLCs) have turned into a well known decision for entrepreneurs because of their adaptable construction and responsibility insurance. Notwithstanding, similar to any business substance, LLCs accompany their own arrangement of benefits and drawbacks. In this exposition, we will investigate the different parts of LLCs and assess both their advantages and downsides.

Advantages:
Restricted Responsibility Security: One of the essential benefits of framing a LLC is the restricted risk insurance it offers to its individuals. This implies that the individual resources of the proprietors, otherwise called individuals, are shielded from the

obligations and liabilities of the organization. In case of claims or loan boss cases, the individual resources of the individuals are for the most part not in danger past their interest in the organization.

Adaptable Administration Construction: LLCs offer adaptability in administration structure, permitting individuals to pick how they maintain that the organization should be made due. They can select a part overseen structure where all individuals take part in the everyday tasks, or they can pick a director oversaw structure where they choose at least one supervisor to maintain the business.

Go Through Tax collection: LLCs appreciate go through tax assessment, and that implies that the organization's benefits and misfortunes are gone through to the singular individuals, who report them on their own expense forms. This evades twofold tax assessment that enterprises frequently face, where benefits are charged at both the corporate and individual levels.

Simple Arrangement and Upkeep: Shaping a LLC is generally simple contrasted with other business substances like companies. The desk work and conventions expected for setting up and keeping an LLC are negligible, making it an appealing choice for private companies and new businesses.

Validity and Amazing skill: Working as an LLC can loan validity and incredible skill to a business. It signs to clients, providers, and financial backers that the organization is a different lawful element and is focused on complying with specific norms and guidelines.

Disadvantages:

Restricted Life expectancy: Dissimilar to companies, which can exist endlessly, LLCs have a restricted life expectancy and may disintegrate upon the demise, withdrawal, or liquidation of a part except if the working understanding indicates in any case. This can present difficulties for long haul business coherence and progression arranging.

Independent work Charges: While LLCs offer pass-through tax collection, individuals are dependent upon independent work charges on their portion of the organization's benefits. This can bring about a higher taxation rate contrasted with being a representative of an organization, where certain expenses are kept at the source.

Intricacy in Expense Treatment: Despite the fact that pass-through tax collection is an advantage of LLCs, it can likewise prompt intricacy in charge treatment, particularly for multi-part LLCs or those with complex proprietorship structures. Individuals might have to explore multifaceted expense rules and guidelines, possibly needing proficient support.

Restricted Raising of Capital: Not at all like enterprises, which can give stock to raise capital, LLCs have restricted choices for raising assets. While they can acquire new individuals or assume obligations, the interaction might be seriously difficult, particularly for new companies or organizations hoping to quickly grow.

State-explicit Guidelines: LLCs are liable to state-explicit guidelines, which can differ essentially contingent upon the locale. This implies that entrepreneurs need to find out more about the regulations and necessities of the state in which they work, adding to the managerial weight and potential consistency costs.

Restricted Risk Organizations (LLCs) offer an adaptable and appealing choice for entrepreneurs looking for obligation security, adaptability in administration, and pass-through tax collection. Notwithstanding, they additionally accompany specific disadvantages, for example, restricted life range, independent work charges, intricacy in charge treatment, restricted raising of capital, and state-explicit guidelines. Prior to framing a LLC, it is fundamental for business visionaries to painstakingly gauge the benefits and detriments and consider talking with lawful and monetary experts to guarantee that it lines up with their business targets and objectives.

°Comparison with Other Business Structures Formation of an LLC

In the immense scene of business substances, the Restricted Obligation Organization (LLC) stands apart as a flexible and famous decision for business visionaries. Its development cycle, advantages, and downsides make it a convincing choice for some. To completely see the value in the arrangement of an LLC, it's vital to balance it with other business structures, in particular sole ownerships, associations, and organizations.

This examination reveals insight into the novel highlights of a LLC and why it very well may be the favored decision for different endeavors.

Sole Ownership: A sole ownership is the least difficult type of business, where an individual works and possesses the whole business. It requires no conventional enrollment, making it simple and cheap to lay out. Nonetheless, the proprietor bears limitless responsibility for the business' obligations and commitments, presenting individual resources for gambles. Also, the sole ownership needs formal design and may confront difficulties in raising capital or extending tasks.

Partnership: Associations come in different structures, including general organizations and restricted organizations. In an overall association, at least two people share possession and the board liabilities, as well as benefits and misfortunes. Like sole ownerships, general organizations offer straightforwardness in line and tax assessment. Nonetheless, accomplices are mutually and severally obligated for the association's obligations, jeopardizing individual resources. Restricted organizations give a level of responsibility insurance for restricted accomplices however expect something like one general cooperate with limitless risk.

Corporation: Dissimilar to sole ownerships and associations, enterprises are lawful elements separate from their proprietors. They offer restricted responsibility security to investors, protecting individual resources from business obligations and liabilities. Companies have a conventional design with investors, chiefs, and officials, giving clear lines of power and responsibility. Notwithstanding, organizations face twofold tax collection, where benefits are charged at both the corporate level and when appropriated to investors as profits. Also, organizations are dependent upon additional administrative necessities and authoritative intricacies.

Restricted Responsibility Organization (LLC): LLCs join the best parts of organizations and enterprises while moderating their disadvantages. Framing a LLC includes recording articles of association with the state and making a working understanding that frames proprietorship, the board, and functional systems. Dissimilar to sole ownerships and organizations, LLCs offer restricted risk insurance to individuals, protecting individual resources from business liabilities. One of the essential benefits of an LLC is its adaptability in tax assessment. Naturally, a LLC is burdened as a pass-through element, significant benefits and misfortunes move through to the individuals' very own expense forms, staying away from twofold tax collection. In any case, LLCs can choose to be burdened as companies if gainful for their particular conditions.

One more key advantage of an LLC is its adaptable administration structure. Individuals can decide to deal with the LLC themselves or select supervisors to deal with everyday tasks. This adaptability takes into account altered administration courses of action custom fitted to the requirements of the business and its individuals.

Furthermore, LLCs offer straightforwardness in consistency and organization contrasted with companies. There are less administrative necessities, negligible customs, and less authoritative weight, making LLCs an alluring choice for private ventures and new companies. Notwithstanding, LLCs might confront difficulties in raising capital contrasted with partnerships, as they can't give stock to raise reserves.

Moreover, while LLCs offer restricted risk insurance, there are occurrences where courts might penetrate the corporate shroud and expect individuals by and by to take responsibility, like deceitful or criminal operations.

The development of a LLC presents a convincing choice for business visionaries looking for an equilibrium of obligation security, adaptability, and straightforwardness. By contrasting LLCs and other business structures, it becomes clear that they offer a one of a kind mix of benefits, making them reasonable for a great many endeavors. Understanding the development interaction and attributes of a LLC engages business people to pursue informed choices that line up with their business objectives and targets. Whether beginning another endeavor or rebuilding a current business, the LLC gives a flexible and compelling arrangement in the present unique business climate.

CHAPTER 2 STEPS TO FORMING AN LLC

Framing a Restricted Risk Organization (LLC) is an essential choice for business people and entrepreneurs looking for lawful insurance, adaptability, and expense benefits. LLCs strike a balance between the simplicity of a partnership and the limited liability protection of a corporation. The most common way of shaping an LLC includes a few stages, each significant for laying out the substance's lawful system and functional design. The entire process of forming an LLC, from initial planning to official registration and beyond, is outlined in detail below.

Stage 1: Exploration and Arranging Research and preparation are essential prior to beginning the LLC formation process.

Think about the accompanying key perspectives:

Business Name: Pick a special and recognizable name for your LLC that consents to your state's naming guidelines. Guarantee the name isn't now being used by another business element. Establish whether an LLC is the best business structure for your requirements. Consider liability protection, taxation, and management flexibility when comparing LLCs to other options like sole proprietorship, partnership, or corporation.

Working Understanding: While not required in all states, it is energetically prescribed to draft a working arrangement. This archive frames the LLC's possession structure, part liabilities, benefit circulation, and functional techniques.

Second Step: Select a Registered Agent Each LLC should have an enlisted specialist, otherwise called a legal specialist or specialist for administration of cycle. On behalf of the LLC, the registered agent is in charge of receiving official correspondence, tax notices, and legal documents. The specialist should include an actual location inside the condition of development and be accessible during normal business hours.

Step 3: File Organizational Documents The Articles of Association, once in a while called a Testament of Development or Endorsement of Association, is the conventional report expected to lay out an LLC with the state.

This archive normally incorporates: LLC name and address Enrolled specialist's name and address The board structure (part oversaw or supervisor made due) The LLC's duration (permanent or limited) Document the Articles of Association with the proper state organization, normally the Secretary of State or

Branch of State, alongside the expected recording charge. A few states offer internet recording choices for comfort.

Stage 4: Acquire an EIN A Business Recognizable proof Number (EIN), otherwise called a Government Duty ID Number, is expected for charge purposes, banking, and recruiting workers. You can get an EIN for your LLC from the Interior Income Administration (IRS) free of charge by applying on the web, via mail, fax, or telephone.

Stage 5: Draft a Working Understanding Albeit not obligatory in all states, drafting a working understanding is energetically suggested for LLCs with various individuals. This archive frames the proprietorship structure, the board liabilities, dynamic cycles, benefit dispersion, and techniques for question goals.

Stage 6: Conform to State and Nearby Prerequisites Contingent upon your area and industry, your LLC might have to acquire extra licenses, grants, or enrollments to lawfully work. Research and conform to all state and neighborhood prerequisites, including drafting regulations, permits to operate, deals, charge grants, and expert licenses.

Stage 7: Open a Business Financial balance For liability protection and financial transparency, it is essential to separate your personal and business finances. In the name of your LLC, open a business bank account and only use it for business transactions. Additionally, this will simplify tax and accounting reporting significantly.

Stage 8: Satisfy Progressing Consistence Commitments In order to keep your LLC legal and in good standing, you must fulfill ongoing compliance obligations. These commitments might include: Recording yearly reports or explanations with the state paying franchise or state taxes annually Holding standard gatherings and keeping precise records Refreshing part or administrator data on a case by case basis.

Step 9: Get the necessary insurance for your business While LLCs offer restricted obligation security, it's as yet reasonable to acquire business protection to defend against surprising dangers and liabilities. You might need property insurance, general liability insurance, or professional liability insurance, depending on your industry and location.

Stage 10: Look for Proficient Direction Exploring the most common way of framing a LLC can be perplexing, particularly while considering legitimate, charge, and administrative ramifications. Think about looking for proficient direction from lawyers, bookkeepers, or business guides who spend significant time in LLC development and private venture matters. Your company's structure can be optimized for long-term success, minimize risks, and ensure compliance with their expertise.

Taking everything into account, framing a LLC includes cautious preparation, adherence to lawful necessities, and continuous consistency endeavors. By following these means and looking for proper direction, you can lay out a strong starting point for your business, appreciate restricted risk insurance, and seek after your innovative objectives with certainty.

°Choosing a Name and Registered Agent

Beginning a Restricted Obligation Organization (LLC) marks the start of an enterprising excursion loaded up with energy and potential. Choosing a suitable name for your LLC and naming a registered agent are two crucial first steps in this process. The foundation for your company's identity, legal standing, and operational efficiency is laid by these decisions, which are more than just administrative responsibilities. We discuss the significance of selecting an LLC's registered agent and name in this comprehensive guide, outlining important considerations and best practices.

Significance of Picking a Name: Choosing the right name for your LLC is something beyond picking something snappy or significant. It fills in as the essential identifier for your business and can altogether affect its prosperity.

Here's the reason it makes a difference:

Brand Character: Your LLC's name is in many cases the primary resource between your business and likely clients. A well-chosen name can help you stand out in a crowded market by conveying your brand's values, personality, and offerings.

Legitimate Consistence: The name you pick should agree with state guidelines, remembering remarkable naming prerequisites and limitations for specific words or expressions. Inability to comply with these principles could bring about deferrals or dismissal during the enlistment cycle.

Brand name Security: A novel and recognizable name diminishes the gamble of encroachment on existing brand names, defending your image's standing and forestalling lawful debates down the line.

Advertising and Website optimization: A Website design enhancement agreeable name can improve your internet based perceivability and make it simpler for expected clients to track down your business through web crawlers and online registries.

Key Contemplations for Picking a Name: Consider the following when coming up with names for your LLC to ensure that you make an educated choice:

Pertinence: Pick a name that mirrors your business' fundamental beliefs, industry, and contributions. Names that are generic or misleading may cause customers to become confused and limit the potential of your brand.

Accessibility: Direct an exhaustive hunt to confirm the accessibility of your ideal name. Check with the Secretary of State's office or online business substance data sets to guarantee no other element is involving a comparative name in your purview.

Space Accessibility: In the present computerized age, getting a matching space name is fundamental for laying out a firm web-based presence. Actually look at space accessibility to guarantee consistency across your site, email, and showcasing materials.

Future Expansion: Consider the name's long-term viability. Will customers still respond to it as your company expands and diversifies its offerings? Choose a name that can be changed and scaled up.

Picking an Enrolled Specialist: A registered agent, also known as a statutory agent or agent for service of process, must be appointed by every LLC. The LLC's official point of contact for correspondence pertaining to legal and administrative matters is the registered agent.

Here's the reason choosing the right enlisted specialist is pivotal:

Legitimate Consistence: State regulations order that LLCs keep an enlisted specialist with an actual location inside the locale where the business is enrolled. Inability to assign an enrolled specialist or keep a legitimate location can bring about punishments, fines, or even the disintegration of your LLC.

Security and privacy: A registered agent keeps your personal information out of public records, giving business owners additional security and privacy. Authoritative reports and official correspondence are conveyed to the enlisted specialist's location, guaranteeing privacy and consistency with administrative prerequisites.

Accessibility: Important documents like legal notices, tax forms, and official correspondence from government agencies can only be received by your registered agent during regular business hours. Pick an enrolled specialist who can speedily advance these records to you, guaranteeing ideal reaction and consistency with cutoff times.

The Selection of a Registered Agent: While choosing an enrolled specialist for your LLC, think about the accompanying standards to go with an educated decision:

Reliability: Select a registered agent whose responsiveness and dependability have been demonstrated in the past. They ought to be open during business hours and able to instantly send any correspondence to you.

Physical Presence: Make certain that the registered agent of your LLC has a physical address in the jurisdiction where it is registered. A PO Box or virtual office may not fulfill the legitimate prerequisites for an enrolled specialist's location. Integrity and professionalism are essential because your registered agent is your company's official spokesperson. Select a registered agent service or an individual with prior experience handling administrative and legal documents.

Flexibility: Consider whether the registered agent provides additional services or support, such as document storage, mail forwarding, or assistance with compliance. Your business's operations can be streamlined and your customer experience can be improved with flexibility and added value. Moves toward Assign an Enlisted Specialist: Whenever you've picked an enrolled specialist for your LLC, follow these moves toward authoritatively assign them: Remember Specialist Data for Articles of Association: While recording your LLC's Articles of Association with the Secretary of State or important state organization, give the name and address of your picked enrolled specialist. The official records of your company will contain this information.

Keep up with Exact Records: Keep definite records of your enrolled specialist's contact data, including any progressions or updates to their location or contact subtleties. Inability to keep up with precise records could bring about missed correspondence or consistency issues.

Reestablishment and Updates: Intermittently survey and update your enrolled specialist data on a case by case basis, particularly in the event that there are changes to your work locale or the enlisted specialist's accessibility. Most states require LLCs to restore their enlisted specialist assignment every year or biennially.

Choosing a registered agent and name for your LLC are crucial decisions that require careful consideration. By choosing a significant and consistent name and assigning a dependable enrolled specialist, you establish a strong starting point for your business' prosperity and life span. Set aside some margin to explore and assess your choices, guaranteeing that your decisions line up with your image's personality, lawful commitments, and functional requirements. You can begin your entrepreneurial journey with confidence and clarity if you have the appropriate registered agent and name.

ºArticles of Organization

Due to their adaptability, tax advantages, and liability protection, Limited Liability Companies (LLCs) have emerged as a popular option for business owners and entrepreneurs. The Articles of Organization, a foundational document that outlines essential information about the company and its structure, are at the center of every LLC formation. In this thorough aide, we will dig into the complexities of Articles of Association, investigating their motivation, key parts, documenting prerequisites, and importance in the domain of business substances.

Reason for Articles of Association: The Articles of Association act as the authority sanction that lays out the presence of a LLC. To formally establish the business, this document is submitted to the appropriate state authority, typically the Secretary of State's office. It describes the LLC's name, purpose, duration (if applicable), registered agent, members, and management structure, among other important information.

Basically, the Articles of Association give an outline to the association's activity and administration.

Key Parts of Articles of Association
Name of the LLC: The LLC's legal name must be included in the Articles of Organization and must comply with the state's naming requirements. The name as a rule incorporates an assignment, for example, "Restricted Risk Organization," "LLC," or a condensing thereof.

Enlisted Specialist: Each LLC should assign an enrolled specialist who is liable for getting authoritative records and official correspondence for the benefit of the organization. The enlisted specialist's name and address should be determined in the Articles of Association.

The LLC's purpose: While some states require a specific statement of purpose, others permit a clause with a broad business purpose. The primary activities or goals for which the LLC is being formed are outlined in this section. Duration: Unless dissolved, most limited liability companies (LLCs) are created with a perpetual duration. However, some limited liability companies (LLCs) may have a predetermined duration, after which they will dissolve by default unless the members decide to extend it.

The executives Construction: The Articles of Association should show how the LLC will be made due. LLCs can be overseen either by their individuals (part made due) or by designated supervisors (chief made due). Who will have authority to make decisions and run the company's business affairs is defined in this section.

Individuals: The Articles of Association normally list the underlying individuals or proprietors of the LLC. Members are people or organizations with ownership stakes in the business. Additionally, the percentage of ownership held by each member may be specified in the Articles in some instances.

Recording Data: The archive should incorporate fundamental documenting data, for example, the date of documenting, the name and mark of the individual or substance presenting the Articles, and any recording expenses expected by the state. Documenting Necessities and Techniques A crucial step in the formation of an LLC is submitting its Articles of Organization, which must be completed in accordance with the state's laws. While explicit prerequisites might shift from one state to another, the general cycle regularly includes the accompanying advances: Name

Accessibility Check: Prior to setting up the Articles of Association, it is prudent to lead a name accessibility check to guarantee that the ideal name for the LLC isn't as of now being used by one more business substance in the state. The Articles of Organization can be drafted once the name has been confirmed. A member of the LLC or a professional service provider, such as an attorney or online legal service, can typically prepare this document. The Articles of Organization must be submitted to the appropriate state agency, typically the Secretary of State's office, along with any applicable filing fees. A few states consider web based recording, while others might require accommodation via mail or face to face.

Distribution Prerequisites (if relevant): In certain states, recently shaped LLCs are expected to distribute a notification of their development in a nearby paper. This necessity is intended to give public notification of the LLC's presence.

Acquiring a Business Recognizable proof Number (EIN): After the Articles of Association are recorded and endorsed, the LLC ought to get a Business ID Number (EIN) from the Inward Income Administration (IRS). An EIN is vital for charge purposes and is utilized to distinguish the LLC in its dealings with the IRS.

Working Understanding: While not a recording prerequisite, it is enthusiastically prescribed for LLCs to take on a working understanding, which is an authoritative report that frames the interior tasks, the executives construction, and possession interests of the organization. This report is regularly made by the individuals and oversees the expectations of the individuals and administrators. Meaning of Articles of Association An LLC's Articles of Organization serve a number of important purposes and are crucial to its existence.

Lawful Presence: By documenting the Articles of Association, the LLC formally appears as a legitimate substance separate from its proprietors. This shields the members' personal assets from the company's debts and liabilities and provides the company with limited liability protection.

Clarity and Structure: The LLC's Articles of Organization clarify the organization's structure and governance, assisting in the prevention of member misunderstandings and disagreements. By illustrating key arrangements, for example, the executives structure, part privileges, and dynamic cycles, the record lays out a system for the activity of the organization.

Consistence: Documenting the Articles of Association guarantees that the LLC is consistent with state regulation necessities for business arrangement. Inability to appropriately record this archive or stick to documenting methods could bring about punishments, fines, or even the nullification of the LLC's legitimate status.

Public Notice: The filing of the Articles of Organization serves as public notice of the LLC's formation in states with publication requirements, informing creditors, customers, and other interested parties of the company's existence. The Articles of Organization serve as the foundation for various business transactions, including opening bank accounts, entering into contracts, obtaining financing, and carrying out other official business activities on the LLC's behalf.

The Articles of Association are the foundation of Restricted Responsibility Organizations, giving the system to their reality, activity, and administration. Entrepreneurs can establish their businesses with confidence knowing that they have established a solid foundation for success by carefully drafting and filing this document in accordance with state law requirements. From characterizing the organization's motivation to determining its administration construction and part freedoms, the Articles of Association assume an essential part in molding the personality and direction of a LLC.

°Legal and Regulatory Considerations

Restricted Risk Organizations (LLCs) have become progressively well known among business visionaries and entrepreneurs because of their adaptability, tax cuts, and restricted responsibility security. However, there is a complicated web of legal and regulatory considerations to navigate when forming and operating an LLC. In this thorough aide, we will investigate the vital lawful and administrative parts of LLCs, including arrangement, administration, tax collection, and consistency.

Establishment of LLCs: Selecting a suitable business name and submitting articles of organization to the appropriate state agency are the first steps in forming an LLC. These articles commonly incorporate fundamental data like the LLC's name, address, enrolled specialist, and reason. The process of formation is governed by state laws, and requirements may differ from jurisdiction to jurisdiction.

Working Understanding: Although it is not always required, LLCs should have an operating agreement because it lays out the business's structure, management, and operations. This internal document aids in the clarification of member rights and responsibilities, profit and loss allocation, decision-making procedures, and dispute resolution strategies.

Protection from Liability Limits: The limited liability protection that an LLC provides to its members is one of the primary advantages. This implies that the individual resources of individuals are for the most part protected from the obligations and liabilities of the business. Nonetheless, it's fundamental to keep up with appropriate corporate customs and try not to blend individual and business funds to safeguard this insurance.

Taxation: LLCs are regularly burdened as pass-through substances, implying that benefits and misfortunes are gone through to the individuals' singular government forms. Nonetheless, LLCs have the adaptability to pick how they need to be burdened, either as a sole ownership, organization, S enterprise, or C partnership. In terms of compliance requirements, tax treatment, and profit distribution, each tax structure has its own implications.

Requirements for Complying: LLCs are dependent upon different consistency commitments at the government, state, and some of the time nearby levels. These might include making annual filings, paying state taxes, keeping accurate records, holding regular meetings, and adhering to rules that are specific to your industry. Inability to meet these commitments can bring about punishments, fines, or even disintegration of the LLC. Aspects of

Regulation: LLCs should stick to administrative necessities forced by government and state organizations relying upon the idea of their business exercises. These guidelines might cover regions like ecological insurance, word related security, shopper assurance, permitting, and allows. To avoid legal repercussions, LLCs must keep up with regulatory changes and ensure compliance.

Worker Relations: The minimum wage, overtime pay, workplace safety, anti discrimination, and employee benefits are just a few of the labor laws that an LLC must follow if it has employees. In addition, LLCs may be required to adhere to regulations regarding employee rights and hiring, firing, and workers' compensation insurance.

Protection of Intellectual Property: LLCs need to protect their licensed innovation freedoms, including brand names, copyrights, licenses, and proprietary advantages. Enrolling brand names and copyrights can give lawful security against encroachment and unapproved use by contenders. Implementing confidentiality and non-disclosure agreements can also assist in safeguarding valuable trade secrets and proprietary data.

Authoritative Commitments: As part of their business operations, LLCs frequently enter into contracts with customers, landlords, suppliers, vendors, and other parties. Contracts must be carefully reviewed and negotiated to ensure that they are favorable and in line with the LLC's interests. Contract violations can result in disagreements, litigation, and financial obligations.

Leave Methodologies: LLCs need to plan for the future, and this includes thinking about ways to get out, like dissolving, selling assets, merging, or buying another company. The procedures for winding up the business and distributing assets in the event of dissolution ought to be outlined in the operating agreement. Members' buy-sell agreements can also address succession planning and ownership interest transfers.

To ensure compliance, reduce risks, and safeguard the business and its members' interests, running an LLC necessitates paying close attention to legal and regulatory considerations. LLCs can better navigate the legal landscape and position themselves for long-term success in the competitive business environment of today by comprehending the complexities of formation, governance, taxation, compliance, and risk management.

CHAPTER 3
OPERATING

AGREEMENT

A working understanding is a critical record for restricted risk organizations (LLCs), filling in as the foundation of the organization's design and tasks. Even though an operating agreement is not required by law in every state, it is strongly suggested that every LLC have one to define the roles, responsibilities, and relationships between members and managers. The LLC's management, ownership, decision-making procedures, financial matters, dispute resolution procedures, and more are all covered in this comprehensive document. Motivation behind a Working Arrangement: Characterizing Proprietorship and Participation: The working understanding determines the possession interests of every part and layouts the cycle for conceding new individuals or moving proprietorship interests. It additionally addresses the limitations of individuals, including their democratic power and benefit dispersions.

The executives Design: It frames the administration construction of the LLC, whether it's part overseen or administrator made due. In a part overseen LLC, all individuals take part in the dynamic cycle, while in a supervisor overseeing LLC, individuals select at least one chief to deal with day to day tasks.

Processes for Making Decisions: The agreement outlines the procedures for making decisions within the LLC, including whether they are made by simple majority vote, unanimous consent, or some other method. It likewise determines which choices require the assent of all individuals and which can be made by an assigned director or chiefs.

Assignment of Benefits and Misfortunes: It frames how benefits and misfortunes will be distributed among individuals, which may not really be relative to their possession advantages. This clause is very important for figuring out how much each member gets out of the profits or losses the company makes.

Capital Contributions: Each member's initial capital contributions and any subsequent contributions are outlined in the agreement. It might likewise indicate the ramifications for neglecting to make required commitments, for example, weakening of possession interests or withdrawal from the LLC.

Appropriations: It determines the timing and strategy for benefit disseminations to individuals, whether as money, property, or different resources. Depending on the terms of the agreement, distributions can be made on a regular schedule or as needed.

Jobs and Obligations: The understanding characterizes the jobs and obligations of individuals and administrators, including their power to tie the LLC in agreements and other lawful arrangements. It also explains how managers and officers can be appointed or removed.

Non-Compete and Confidentiality: In order to safeguard the LLC's intellectual property, trade secrets, and competitive advantages, some operating agreements include provisions regarding confidentiality, non-compete clauses, and non-solicitation agreements.

Question Goal: in case of debates among individuals or among individuals and administrators, the working understanding might incorporate arrangements for intervention, mediation, or other elective debate goal components to determine clashes genially and productively.

Disintegration and Liquidation: It tends to the strategies for dissolving the LLC, including the dispersion of resources for individuals and the installment of remarkable obligations and commitments. The steps to be taken in the event of the LLC's termination are detailed in this crucial section. Why an Operating Agreement Is Essential:

Legal Protection: By clearly defining the LLC's and its members' rights, responsibilities, and expectations, an operating agreement provides legal protection. It forestalls errors and questions that might emerge without any composed documentation.

Lucidity and Assurance: By framing the standards and methods overseeing the LLC's activities, a working arrangement gives clearness and sureness to all partners. It guarantees that everybody is in total agreement viewing central questions like administration, proprietorship, and direction.

Adaptability: Working arrangements are profoundly adjustable, permitting LLCs to fit the record to their particular requirements and inclinations. The LLC's specific circumstances can be reflected in the agreement's allocation of profits, defining voting rights, and management roles.

Protection of Minority Interests: Without adequate safeguards, minority members of multi-member LLCs may be at risk of being marginalized or disadvantaged. By defining voting thresholds, consent requirements, and dispute resolution procedures that guarantee fair treatment for all members, an operating agreement can safeguard minority interests.

Enhanced Credibility: The LLC's credibility in the eyes of third parties, such as investors, lenders, suppliers, and customers, is enhanced by a well-drafted operating agreement. It exhibits that the organization is expertly overseen and has clear approaches and methods set up.

Compliance with State Law: While the majority of states do not require LLCs to have an operating agreement, some, like California and New York, strongly encourage it. Indeed, even in states where it's not obligatory, having a working arrangement can assist LLCs show consistency with state regulation and keep away from expected lawful difficulties.

Preservation of Limited Liability: By ensuring that the business is run in accordance with legal requirements, operating agreements can help preserve the limited liability protection afforded to LLC members. By outlining the division among individual and business resources, the arrangement helps safeguard individuals from individual risk for the LLC's obligations and commitments. Key Contemplations While Drafting a Working Arrangement:

Conference with Legitimate Direction: It's fitting to look for the direction of a certified lawyer experienced in business regulation while drafting a working understanding. Legitimate advice can guarantee that the arrangement conforms to state regulation, resolves generally important issues, and safeguards the interests of the LLC and its individuals.

Lucidity and Accuracy: The working arrangement ought to be written in clear, succinct language that is straightforward for all gatherings included. Equivocalness and unclearness ought to be kept away from to forestall false impressions and questions from now on.

Flexibility for Future Changes: The LLC's operating agreement should be clear and precise, but it should also be flexible enough to accommodate future circumstances changes. Arrangements for correcting the understanding ought to be incorporated to work with refreshes depending on the situation.

Thorough Inclusion: The working understanding ought to address all vital parts of the LLC's tasks, including the executives, proprietorship, direction, monetary issues, debate goal, and disintegration. There should be no significant issue left unresolved. Before the operating agreement is finalized and signed by all LLC members, it is essential to ensure that they are in agreement with its terms. Depending on the terms of the agreement, either unanimous consent or majority approval may be required.

Normal Audit and Updates: Working arrangements ought to be explored occasionally and refreshed as important to reflect changes in the LLC's design, participation, or working circumstances. The agreement stays relevant and effective over time with regular review.

Consistence with State Regulation: The working understanding ought to conform to the regulations and guidelines administering LLCs in the state where the organization is enlisted. State-explicit necessities ought to be painstakingly thought of and integrated into the arrangement depending on the situation.

An LLC's operating agreement serves as a foundation for the company's governance, management, and operations. The agreement contributes to the achievement of clarity, certainty, and legal protection for all parties involved by defining ownership interests, management structure, decision-making procedures, and other essential aspects of the business. While not generally lawfully required, having a very much drafted working understanding is firmly prescribed for each LLC to moderate dangers, forestall debates, and work with smooth tasks.

When drafting or revising an operating agreement, it is essential to consult with legal counsel to ensure compliance with state law and the protection of the LLC's interests.

°State Regulation

In the United States, Limited Liability Companies (LLCs) are based on state regulations, which serve as their legal foundation. Each state has its own arrangement of regulations administering the development, activity, and disintegration of LLCs, mirroring the assorted requirements and needs of nearby organizations and economies. Understanding these guidelines is critical for business visionaries and entrepreneurs hoping to lay out and deal with an LLC. In this thorough aide, we will investigate the vital parts of state guidelines on LLCs, including development prerequisites, the executives designs, tax collection, and continuous consistency commitments.

Arrangement Necessities: The first step in forming an LLC is to submit the required paperwork to the state government. Despite the fact that state-specific requirements vary, the following elements are consistent:

Name Reservation: Prior to recording articles of association, many states require the candidate to save the ideal LLC name for a specific period. The name should consent to state rules, normally keeping away from terms that suggest the element is a company or government office.

Articles of Organization: Filed with the state's secretary of state or equivalent agency is this document, also known as a certificate of formation or certificate of organization. It normally incorporates essential data like the LLC's name, address, enrolled specialist, reason, and the executives structure.

Registered Agent: Most states require LLCs to appoint a registered agent, who acts as the company's official contact for legal matters. The enrolled specialist should have an actual location in the state where the LLC is framed and be accessible during normal business hours.

Working Understanding: Albeit not generally legally necessary, a working arrangement is a critical inside record that frames the possession structure, the board liabilities, benefit circulation, and dynamic cycles of the LLC. While certain states permit oral working arrangements, a composed understanding is strongly suggested for lucidity and legitimate insurance.

The board Designs: LLCs offer adaptability in picking their administration structure, permitting individuals to work the business straightforwardly or name administrators to supervise everyday tasks. State guidelines commonly perceive two administration structures:

Member-Managed LLC: In a member-managed LLC, each member can participate in the company's management and decision-making processes. This construction is normal in private ventures and new companies where individuals are effectively associated with tasks.

Chief Oversaw LLC: In a director oversaw LLC, the executives authority is designated to at least one delegated supervisors, who could possibly be individuals from the LLC. When there are passive investors or when members lack the expertise or time to oversee operations, this structure is frequently chosen.

Taxation: LLCs benefit from pass-through taxation, which means that profits and losses are taxed at the member level rather than the entity level. In any case, state tax assessment from LLCs fluctuates altogether, for certain states forcing extra expenses or charges.

Key contemplations include:

State Personal Duty: Most states demand annual assessment on LLCs in view of the element's available pay. LLCs must be aware of their state's tax laws and obligations because the rates and brackets vary from state to state.

Establishment Duty or Yearly Report Charges: Many states require LLCs to pay a yearly establishment assessment or record a yearly report to keep up with great standing. How much expense or charge normally relies upon variables like the LLC's income or total assets.

Sales and Use Tax: LLCs that sell goods or services may be required to pay sales and use taxes in their respective states. Consistency with these commitments requires enlisting with the state charge authority, gathering and transmitting deals expense, and recording intermittent returns.

Business Charges: LLCs with representatives should keep and transmit finance assessments to the state, including personal duty keeping, joblessness protection expense, and state incapacity protection charge.

Obligations for Continuous Compliance: Once shaped, LLCs should follow different continuous commitments to keep up with their legitimate status and great remaining with the state.

These responsibilities might include:

Yearly Filings: Many states require LLCs to record a yearly report or explanation of data with the secretary of state's office. Most of the time, the information in this report about the LLC's members, managers, and registered agent is up to date. Licenses and Permits for Businesses Depending on the nature of the LLC's business activities, it may be necessary to obtain specific state or local licenses and permits. Professional licenses, zoning permits, health permits, and sales tax permits are typical examples.

Requirements for Meetings: Holding regular meetings of members or managers can help ensure proper communication, decision-making, and documentation of crucial business matters, though it is not always required.

Recordkeeping: Most of the time, limited liability companies (LLCs) are required to keep accurate and current records of corporate documents, financial transactions, meeting minutes, and other important records. To demonstrate compliance with state regulations and make it easier to file taxes, good record keeping is essential.

Specific Rules for Each State: LLCs may be governed by state-specific requirements and nuances in addition to these general rules. For instance:

California: LLCs in California are dependent upon a yearly least establishment charge in light of all out pay.

New York: LLCs in New York should distribute a notification of development in assigned papers in no less than 120 days of development.

Nevada: Nevada is known for its good business climate, with no state corporate annual expense, major areas of strength for and assurances for LLC proprietors. LLCs must thoroughly investigate and comprehend the state-specific regulations and requirements in which they operate or are considering forming.

State guidelines on LLCs assume a crucial part in molding the legitimate structure for these flexible business substances. Understanding and adhering to state laws is essential for the successful operation of an LLC, from formation requirements to ongoing compliance obligations. By exploring the administrative scene successfully, business people and entrepreneurs can use the advantages of restricted obligation insurance, adaptable administration designs, and pass-through tax assessment presented by LLCs to accomplish their business objectives.

°Compliance Requirements

Due to their adaptability, simplicity, and liability protection, Limited Liability Companies (LLCs) are a popular business entity for entrepreneurs. Notwithstanding, similar to some other business structures, LLCs should stick to different consistency prerequisites to keep up with their legitimate standing and safeguard the interests of their partners. In this talk, we dive into the mind boggling scene of consistency prerequisites for LLCs, investigating key perspectives, suggestions, and best practices.

Grasping LLCs: Prior to diving into consistency necessities, getting a handle on the major idea of LLCs is critical. A LLC joins the restricted risk security of an enterprise with the pass-through tax collection from an organization or sole ownership. Members, the owners of this distinctive hybrid structure, are shielded from personal responsibility for the obligations and debts of the business.

Registration and Formation: The filing of articles of organization with the appropriate state authority is the first step in forming an LLC. For LLC formation, each state has its own requirements and procedures. Typically, a formal document outlining key details like the company's name, address, purpose, management structure, and registered agent must be submitted.

Consistence Tip: Guarantee consistency with state-explicit arrangement prerequisites and give close consideration to cut off times and documenting charges to keep away from likely punishments or postponements.

Contract of Operation: While not generally a lawful prerequisite, drafting a working understanding is energetically suggested for LLCs. This record frames the inside activities of the organization, including the board structure, part expectations, benefit appropriation, casting a ballot methodology, and debate goal components.

Compliance Tip: Even though it is not required in every state, having a comprehensive operating agreement can help keep members from misunderstanding each other and fighting, making business operations run more smoothly.

Taxation: LLCs benefit from pass-through taxation, which means that members' individual tax returns receive profits and losses instead of corporate taxation. Be that as it may, LLCs should in any case follow government, state, and neighborhood charge regulations, including recording yearly expense forms and settling any relevant duties. A tax professional can help you comply with your responsibilities and make the most of any available tax deductions and credits.

Permits to operate and Allows: Contingent upon the idea of the LLC's business exercises and its area, getting explicit licenses and allows might be important to legitimately work. These may incorporate general permits to operate, industry-explicit licenses, wellbeing grants, drafting grants, and that's just the beginning.

Compliance Tip: Before beginning operations, research the licensing requirements that apply to your industry and location and obtain all necessary permits to avoid paying fines or facing legal consequences.

Yearly Revealing and Expenses: To maintain their active status, LLCs must file annual reports and pay the associated fees in many states. These reports commonly update the state on the organization's ongoing data, like location, individuals, and the board structure.

Consistence Tip: Monitor yearly report cutoff times and guarantee convenient accommodation to keep away from punishments or regulatory disintegration.

Record-Keeping: Financial transactions, meeting minutes, member agreements, tax filings, and other important documents must be kept up to date and accurate by LLCs. Great record-keeping guarantees consistency as well as works with straightforwardness and responsibility inside the organization.

Consistence Tip: Carry out a vigorous record-keeping framework all along, including both physical and computerized capacity choices, and consistently survey and update records depending on the situation.

Respect for Employment Laws: The minimum wage, overtime pay, workplace safety, anti-discrimination, and employee benefits are just a few of the employment laws that the LLC must abide by if it has employees.

Compliance Tip: Keep up with changes to employment laws and regulations and put policies and procedures into place to make sure you're following them and reduce legal risks.

Formalities of the Company: In terms of corporate formalities, LLCs offer more flexibility than corporations, but certain procedures must still be followed to maintain the company's separation from its owners. This might incorporate holding ordinary gatherings, reporting significant choices, and keeping individual and business funds isolated.

Consistence Tip: Sticking to corporate conventions can assist with saving the restricted risk assurance managed by the LLC structure and forestall "puncturing the corporate cloak" in case of lawful questions.

Consistence prerequisites for LLCs envelop an extensive variety of legitimate, monetary, and functional contemplations. By getting it and perseveringly sticking to these necessities, LLCs can safeguard their legitimate standing, moderate dangers, and cultivate a favorable climate for development and achievement.

When navigating complex compliance issues, LLC owners and stakeholders can gain invaluable support and peace of mind by seeking professional guidance.

°Tax Implications for LLCs

Restricted Risk Organizations (LLCs) have turned into a well known decision of business structure for business people and entrepreneurs because of their adaptability and obligation insurance. Be that as it may, understanding the expense ramifications of working as an LLC is essential for successful monetary preparation and consistency with charge regulations. This thorough aide investigates the different duty contemplations that LLCs should explore, including tax collection at the government, state, and neighborhood levels, as well as methodologies for limiting expense liabilities.

Outline of LLC Tax collection: Dissimilar to organizations, which are liable to twofold tax collection (tax assessment at both the corporate and individual levels), LLCs are thought of as "go through" elements for charge purposes. This implies that the benefits and misfortunes of the business "go through" to the proprietors, who report them on their own assessment forms. Of course, single-part LLCs are burdened as sole ownerships, while multi-part LLCs are burdened as organizations. However, LLCs can choose corporate taxation by submitting Form 8832 to the Internal Revenue Service. LLC individuals are ordinarily viewed as independently employed for charge purposes and should make good on independent work charges, including Government backed retirement and Federal medical care charges, on their portion of the organization's benefits.

Government Tax assessment from LLCs:

Single-part LLCs: The IRS regards single-part LLCs as "dismissed elements," implying that the business' pay and costs are accounted for on Time C of the proprietor's very own government form (Structure 1040). According to the operating agreement for multi-member LLCs, profits and losses are divided among each member in proportion to their ownership percentage. Using Schedule E (Form 1040), members report their share of the income or loss on their individual tax returns. LLCs can likewise choose to be burdened as a S Organization by documenting Structure 2553 with the IRS. Certain tax advantages of an S corporation include the ability to defer self-employment taxes on owner distributions (dividends).

State Tax collection from LLCs: LLCs may be subject to state income taxes, franchise taxes, or other state-level taxes and fees due to the wide range of state tax laws. A few states demand a yearly LLC expense or charge in view of the organization's income or resources. It's fundamental for LLCs to figure out their state's duty prerequisites and consent to all recording commitments.

Nearby Tax collection from LLCs: Notwithstanding government and state charges, LLCs might be dependent upon neighborhood charges, for example, city or region business charges, local charges, or deals charges. LLCs should ensure compliance with local tax regulations and rates by consulting with local tax authorities or a tax professional. Charge

Derivations and Credits for LLCs: LLCs can deduct customary and vital costs of doing business, like lease, utilities, pay rates, and advertising costs, to diminish their available pay. Additionally, LLCs may be eligible for a number of tax credits, such as the Research and Development Tax Credit or the Small Business Health Care Tax Credit, which can help them pay less in taxes overall. To get the most out of tax deductions and credits, it's important to keep accurate records of expenses and proper documentation.

Assessed Duties and Hold back: LLC individuals are liable for paying assessed charges on their portion of the organization's pay consistently, regularly on a quarterly premise. Inability to create assessed charge installments can bring about punishments and interest charges. LLCs ought to work with a duty expert to decide the suitable assessed charge installments in view of their normal pay.

Charge Arranging Techniques for LLCs:

Structuring distributions: LLCs have the ability to strategically divide profits and losses among members in order to achieve the best possible tax outcome, taking into account the particular tax situation of each member.

Retirement arranging: LLC proprietors can add to burden advantaged retirement accounts, for example, SEP-IRAs or Solo 401(k)s, to diminish their available pay and save for retirement.

Devaluation and capital consumptions: LLCs can exploit deterioration derivations and Segment 179 discounting to discount the expense of business resources after some time, decreasing their available pay.

Wellbeing investment accounts (HSAs) and adaptable spending accounts (FSAs): LLC proprietors might be qualified to add to HSAs or FSAs to pay for qualified clinical costs on a pre-charge premise, bringing down their available pay.

Consistence and Announcing Necessities: Depending on their tax classification, LLCs are required to submit Form 1065 (Partnership Return) or Form 1120 (Corporate Return) annual tax returns to the IRS, detailing their income and expenses. Additionally, LLCs may be required to comply with a variety of local reporting and filing requirements as well as state and local tax returns. Resistance with charge regulations can bring about punishments, fines, and other lawful results, so it's fundamental for LLCs to remain informed and satisfy all duty commitments.

Exploring the expense ramifications of working as an LLC requires cautious preparation, consistency with charge regulations, and progressing checking of duty improvements at the government, state, and nearby levels. By figuring out their assessment commitments, utilizing accessible allowances and credits, and executing successful duty arranging systems,

LLCs can limit their expense liabilities and improve their monetary results. Talking with a certified duty expert can give important direction and backing in exploring the perplexing scene of LLC tax collection.

CHAPTER 4 TAX CLASSIFICATION OPTIONS

Due to their adaptability and liability protection, Limited Liability Companies (LLCs) are a popular choice for entrepreneurs and small business owners. The choice of the tax classification, which determines how the business is taxed by the Internal Revenue Service (IRS), is one crucial decision when forming an LLC. Understanding the accessible choices is urgent for upgrading charge productivity and following legitimate necessities. In this exhaustive aide, we'll investigate the different assessment characterization choices for LLCs and their suggestions.

An Overview of the Types of LLC Taxes: For tax purposes, Limited Liability Companies are regarded as "pass-through" entities, meaning that the company itself does not pay taxes. Instead, the owners "pass through" profits and losses to them, who report them on their own tax returns. In any case, LLCs have the adaptability to pick how they need to be burdened.

Default Grouping: Naturally, a solitary part LLC is burdened as a sole ownership, while a multi-part LLC is burdened as an organization. This indicates that the owner(s) must use Schedule C (for sole proprietorships) or Form 1065 (for partnerships) to report income and expenses on their individual tax returns.

Choosing Corporate Tax assessment: LLCs have the choice to choose corporate tax collection by documenting Structure 8832 with the IRS. This permits the LLC to be treated as a C Enterprise or a S Partnership for charge purposes. Some advantages of choosing corporate taxation include lower tax rates for C corporations and pass-through taxation for S corporations.

C Organization Tax assessment: Deciding on C Enterprise tax assessment implies that the LLC is burdened independently from its proprietors. The corporate assessment rate applies to the LLC's benefits, and investors are burdened again on any profits received. While C Partnerships face twofold tax assessment, they offer benefits like restricted obligation assurance and potential expense reserve funds through allowances and credits.

Choice for S Corporation: The LLC must meet certain eligibility requirements, such as having fewer than 100 shareholders and only one stock class, in order to choose S Corporation status. S Enterprises appreciate go through tax assessment, implying that benefits and misfortunes move through to the investors' singular expense forms without being dependent upon corporate duty at the element level. This can bring about critical expense investment funds for qualified LLCs.

Correlation of Expense Arrangements: Each assessment characterization choice enjoys its own benefits and burdens, contingent upon the particular conditions of the LLC and its proprietors. Sole ownership and organization tax assessment are moderately basic and proposition adaptability yet may open proprietors to more noteworthy individual risk. C Partnership tax assessment gives restricted risk security and potential tax breaks yet may bring about twofold tax collection. S Corporation taxation has stricter eligibility requirements but offers the advantages of pass-through taxation with limited liability.

Variables to Consider: The nature of the business, the number of owners, income projections, long-term objectives, and potential tax implications should all be taken into consideration when selecting an LLC's tax classification. Assessing these factors and making an informed decision can be made with the assistance of a tax advisor or accountant.

Changing the Type of Tax: An LLC may benefit from changing its tax status over time in some circumstances. This should be possible by recording the fitting structures with the IRS, for example, Structure 8832 for choosing corporate tax collection or Structure 2553 for S Partnership political decision. However, there are restrictions and deadlines that must be adhered to, so before making any changes, you should talk to a tax professional.

Consistence and Detailing Necessities: No matter what the expense grouping picked, LLCs are dependent upon different consistency and announcing necessities at both the government and state levels. These may include adhering to state-specific regulations, keeping accurate financial records, and filing annual tax returns. Inability to meet these commitments can bring about punishments and legitimate outcomes.

Because it can affect taxation, liability, and overall business strategy, LLCs must make the right tax classification decision. By understanding the accessible choices and their suggestions, LLC proprietors can settle on informed choices that line up with their objectives and boost charge proficiency. Talking with a certified expense counselor or bookkeeper is prescribed to explore the intricacies of duty grouping and guarantee consistency with lawful prerequisites.

The business structure, ownership, income, and long-term goals of an LLC must all be carefully taken into consideration when selecting the appropriate tax classification. By gauging the benefits and burdens of every choice and looking for proficient direction when required, LLC proprietors can pursue informed choices that help their monetary and functional objectives.

°Pass-through Taxation

Go through tax collection is a vital part of Restricted Obligation Organizations (LLCs) in the US, addressing a critical benefit for some organizations. Entrepreneurs and small business owners looking for the most advantageous structure for their ventures need to have a solid understanding of this taxation model. In this thorough investigation, we dig into the complexities of pass-through tax collection for LLCs, its advantages, disadvantages, and key contemplations. What is Pass-through Tax collection? Go through tax assessment alludes to the duty treatment where business benefits are not charged at the substance level yet are rather gone through to the proprietors' singular expense forms. This tax collection model applies to different business structures, including sole ownerships, organizations, S partnerships, and Restricted Obligation Organizations (LLCs). However, LLCs stand out because of their adaptability and liability protection features. For LLCs, how does pass-through taxation work? Pass-through taxation means that LLCs do not pay federal income taxes to the company itself. Instead, the LLC's owners, also known as members, report the profits and losses on their individual tax returns by "passing through" the business entity. The double taxation that is frequently associated with corporations, in which profits are taxed at both the corporate and individual levels, is eliminated by this taxation model.

Pass-through taxation benefits LLCs: Because LLC members only need to report business income and losses on their individual tax returns, pass-through taxation makes tax reporting simpler for them.

Charge Adaptability: LLC individuals can utilize business misfortunes to counterbalance pay from different sources, possibly diminishing their general expense responsibility.

Evasion of Twofold Tax assessment: In contrast to C partnerships, where benefits are charged at both the corporate and individual levels, go through tax assessment guarantees that LLC benefits are just burdened once, at the singular level.

Move Through of Derivations: Derivations and credits accessible to the LLC can course through to the individuals, permitting them to exploit different tax reductions.

Go through of Tax reductions: LLC individuals might be qualified for specific tax breaks connected with the business, which can straightforwardly decrease their duty commitments.

Downsides and Contemplations:

Self-Employment Taxes: Members of an LLC usually have to pay self-employment taxes on their share of the profits of the business. These taxes come from both Social Security and Medicare taxes that are paid by employers and employees.

Annual Assessment Rates: The duty rates applied to LLC benefits went through to individuals rely upon their singular expense sections, which can shift and possibly bring about higher assessment liabilities for higher-pay people. Pass-through taxation can be straightforward for single-member LLCs, but it can become more complicated for multi-member LLCs, particularly when it comes to profit allocation and member distributions.

State Taxes: Depending on the state's tax laws and regulations, LLCs may be subject to state-level taxes.

Chance of Review: LLCs might confront expanded examination from charge specialists because of the potential for misuse or misclassification of pay and costs.

Strategies for Getting the Most Out of It:

Strategic Allocation of Profits and Losses: Members of an LLC can strategically divide profits and losses among themselves in order to achieve the best possible tax outcomes based on their particular tax circumstances.

Utilization of Tax Credits: LLC members' tax liabilities can be further reduced by taking advantage of available tax credits, but careful planning and compliance with relevant tax regulations are required.

Work of Duty Experts: Talking with charge experts can assist LLC individuals with exploring complex expense rules, augment allowances, and guarantee consistence with government and state charge regulations.

Contributions to Retirement Accounts: Contributions to retirement accounts, such as Solo 401(k)s or SEP-IRAs, can help members save for retirement and reduce their current tax obligations all at the same time.

Ordinary Assessment Arranging: Carrying out customary duty arranging techniques can help LLC individuals expect and deal with their expense commitments really, limiting astonishments and upgrading charge effectiveness.

Go through tax collection is a major trait of LLCs that offers various advantages, including effortlessness, charge adaptability, and the evasion of twofold tax collection. Strategic planning and adherence to tax laws can assist LLC members in maximizing benefits and minimizing tax liabilities, despite this taxation model's drawbacks and considerations. Entrepreneurs and owners of small businesses who want to make the most of the advantages of the LLC structure while also getting the best possible tax results need to have a solid understanding of the intricacies of pass-through taxation.

°Tax Deductions and Credits for LLCs

Any business, including Limited Liability Companies (LLCs), relies heavily on tax credits and deductions to manage its finances. Understanding these ideas is fundamental for LLC proprietors to streamline their assessment liabilities and boost their productivity. In this complete aide, we'll dive into the universe of duty allowances and credits for LLCs, investigating the distinctions between the two, normal derivations and credits accessible to LLCs, and methodologies for actually utilizing them.

1. Separating Derivations and Credits: Prior to digging into explicit derivations and credits, recognizing the two is significant. A company's taxable income is reduced by tax deductions, thereby lowering its taxable income. Then again, tax breaks straightforwardly decrease how much duty is owed by the business. While derivations decrease the available pay, credits give a dollar-to dollar decrease in the genuine duty obligation.

2. Normal Assessment Derivations for LLCs: LLCs, as other business substances, are qualified for different duty allowances to bring down their available pay. The absolute most normal derivations for LLCs include:

Operating Expenses: LLCs are able to deduct ordinary and necessary business-related expenses. Rent, utilities, office supplies, salaries, and insurance premiums are all included in this.

Business Travel: Costs connected with business travel, including transportation, housing, and dinners, are by and large deductible. To substantiate these costs, proper documentation must be kept, though.

Depreciation: LLCs can use depreciation to deduct the cost of business assets over their useful lives. This incorporates gear, hardware, vehicles, and other substantial resources utilized in the business.

Work space Derivation: On the off chance that the LLC's chief business environment is a work space, a part of home-related costs, for example, lease, contract interest, utilities, and upkeep might be deductible.

Health care coverage Expenses: LLCs that give health care coverage inclusion to their representatives, including proprietors, can regularly deduct the charges paid for such inclusion.

Interest Costs: Interest paid on business advances, credit extensions, and different types of funding is by and large deductible, dependent upon specific restrictions.

Proficient Charges: Expenses paid to attorneys, bookkeepers, advisors, and other expert specialist organizations for administrations connected with the LLC's business exercises are deductible.

Charitable Contributions: The LLC can typically deduct its contributions to qualified charitable organizations as business expenses.

3. LLCs Receive Tax Benefits: Tax credits provide a more direct benefit by reducing the LLC's actual tax liability, whereas tax deductions are useful for lowering taxable income.

Some normal tax breaks accessible to LLCs include:

Small Business Health Care Tax Credit: LLCs that offer health insurance to their employees may be eligible for the Small Business Health Care Tax Credit if they meet certain requirements, such as having fewer than 25 full-time equivalent employees and paying a minimum percentage of premiums for their employees.

Work Opportunity Tax Credit (WOTC): The WOTC gives businesses, like LLCs, that hire people from certain groups, like veterans, ex-offenders, and people who get certain kinds of government help, a tax credit.

Innovative work (Research and development)

Tax reduction: LLCs that take part in qualified innovative work exercises might be qualified for a tax break in view of a level of their qualified Research and development consumptions.

Tax Credits for Energy Efficiency: LLCs that make investments in property or equipment that uses less energy may be able to take advantage of tax breaks designed to encourage energy efficiency and long-term sustainability.

Disabled Access Credit: LLCs may be eligible for the Disabled Access Credit if they spend money to make their businesses more accessible to people with disabilities.

4. Techniques for Boosting Assessment Derivations and Credits: To enhance their duty position, LLC proprietors can utilize different methodologies to expand derivations and credits: Keep Nitty gritty Records: Keeping up with precise and itemized records of all costs of doing business is vital for validating derivations and credits asserted on the expense form.

Make Use of Retirement Plans: LLCs can potentially take advantage of tax breaks by contributing to retirement plans like SEP-IRAs, SIMPLE IRAs, or 401(k) plans.

Consider Substance Design: Contingent upon the conditions, LLC proprietors might profit from choosing an alternate expense order for their business, for example, S partnership status, which can influence the accessibility of specific derivations and credits.

Remain Informed: Duty regulations and guidelines are likely to change, so it's fundamental for LLC proprietors to remain informed about advancements that might influence their assessment arranging systems.

5. **Discussion with Duty Experts:** Given the intricacy of duty regulations and the possible outcomes of stumbles, LLC proprietors are urged to look for direction from qualified charge experts, like ensured public bookkeepers (CPAs) or assessment lawyers. These experts can give customized guidance custom-made to the particular requirements and conditions of the LLC, assisting with guaranteeing consistency with charge regulations and improvement of assessment derivations and credits.

Charge derivations and credits offer important open doors for LLCs to limit their duty liabilities and upgrade their monetary presentation. By figuring out the differentiations among derivations and credits, recognizing qualified expenses, and executing powerful assessment arranging systems, LLC proprietors can explore the intricacies of the duty code and position their organizations for progress.

○ Accounting Practices for LLCs

Due to their adaptability, liability protection, and tax advantages, Limited Liability Companies (LLCs) are a popular business structure. Notwithstanding, similar to any business element, LLCs should stick to sound bookkeeping practices to guarantee monetary straightforwardness, consistency, and informed navigation. In this talk, we will dig into the fundamental bookkeeping rehearses custom-made explicitly for LLCs, featuring key standards, detailing necessities, and best practices to upgrade monetary administration.

Laying out Bookkeeping Frameworks:

Choosing a proper bookkeeping strategy: LLCs can pick either cash-premise and accumulation premise bookkeeping. While cash-premise records exchanges when money is gotten or paid, gathering premise perceives income and costs when they are brought about, paying little heed to income. Carrying out bookkeeping programming: Using bookkeeping programming smoothes out accounting processes, works with precise record-keeping, and produces canny monetary reports. Famous choices incorporate QuickBooks, Xero, and FreshBooks.

Keeping your personal and business finances separate:

Open a business ledger: Isolating individual and business funds is urgent for keeping up with LLC's restricted responsibility security and guaranteeing exact monetary detailing.

Try not to intermix reserves: LLC individuals ought to abstain from blending individual costs in with deals to keep up with monetary straightforwardness and work with examining processes.

Documentation and Record-Keeping:

Keep up with definite records: LLCs ought to determinedly record every single monetary exchange, including solicitations, receipts, bank explanations, and agreements, to give an exact portrayal of the organization's monetary wellbeing. Documents should be organized in a methodical way, either digitally or in physical files, to make them easier to find and access during audits or financial analysis.

Planning and Monetary Preparation:

Create a budget: LLCs can improve their revenue forecasts, resource allocation, and cost-optimization strategies by creating a comprehensive budget.

Screen monetary execution: Routinely survey planned versus genuine costs and income to check monetary execution and settle on informed vital choices.

Reporting and compliance with taxes:

Figure out charge commitments: LLCs are dependent upon different duty commitments, including annual expenses, independent work charges, and possibly state-explicit assessments. Talk with charge experts to guarantee consistency.

Document fundamental assessment forms: LLCs should record yearly expense forms, for example, Structure 1065 (Association Return) or Structure 1120 (Corporate Return), contingent upon their duty arrangement. Moreover, LLC individuals might have to record individual expense forms announcing their portion of benefits or misfortunes.

Distributions and Contributions to Capital:

Document capital contributions: LLC members should keep accurate capital accounts by recording all contributions, whether in cash, property, or services. Develop clear guidelines for distributing profits and losses among LLC members to ensure equitable treatment and avoid disputes by establishing distribution policies.

Monetary Revealing:

Prepare financial statements LLCs typically produce three primary financial statements: a cash flow statement, an income statement, and a balance sheet. These reports give partners bits of knowledge into the organization's monetary position, execution, and liquidity.

Modify revealing on a case by case basis: Designer monetary reports to meet the particular necessities of partners, like financial backers, banks, or administrative organizations, by including important measurements and investigations.

Compliance with Requirements of the Law:

Keep up with new regulations: LLCs must abide by federal, state, and local accounting, tax, and business operations regulations. Keep up with changes to the law to ensure compliance and reduce legal risks.

Draw in proficient help if important: Complex administrative prerequisites might require the ability of bookkeeping experts or legitimate advice to successfully explore.

Risk Management and Internal Controls:

Carry out inside controls: Lay out interior control techniques to shield resources, forestall misrepresentation, and guarantee the precision of monetary revealing. Regular audits, authorization protocols, and duties segregation are all examples of this.

Risk assessment and risk mitigation: To safeguard against adverse events like market fluctuations, legal disputes, or operational disruptions, identify potential risks to the LLC's financial stability and implement risk mitigation strategies.

Constant Improvement and Variation: Utilize technological innovations like artificial intelligence, blockchain, and cloud-based accounting solutions to improve accounting processes' efficiency, accuracy, and security.

Continuously evaluate and adapt procedures: In order to drive continuous improvement and optimize financial management, regularly evaluate the efficiency of accounting procedures and practices by incorporating feedback, lessons learned, and industry best practices.

Compelling bookkeeping rehearses are primary to the achievement and manageability of Restricted Obligation Organizations (LLCs). By laying out vigorous bookkeeping frameworks, keeping up with straightforward monetary records, consenting to administrative prerequisites, and embracing consistent improvement, LLCs can upgrade monetary straightforwardness, alleviate chances, and work with informed decision-production to accomplish their business targets. Sticking to sound bookkeeping standards encourages trust among partners, upholds long haul development, and guarantees the thriving of LLCs in an always advancing business scene.

CHAPTER 5
BOOKKEEPING BASICS

Any successful business, including Limited Liability Companies (LLCs), relies heavily on accurate bookkeeping.

Accurate financial records are essential for making well-informed business decisions, complying with tax requirements, and attracting investors.

Proper bookkeeping ensures this. In this extensive aide, we will dig into the major standards of accounting for LLCs, concealing all that from setting your books to overseeing everyday exchanges and planning budget reports.

Figuring out LLCs and their Monetary Construction We will investigate the fundamentals of LLCs in this chapter, including their ownership, financial obligations, and legal structure. We'll talk about how important it is to keep personal and business finances separate, how to choose the right accounting method (cash or accrual), and what equity and liabilities are in an LLC.

Setting Up Your Books Setting up your books appropriately is fundamental for exact record-keeping. This part will direct you through the most common way of making a diagram of records custom fitted to your LLC's particular requirements. We'll talk about how crucial it is to correctly classify transactions, set up a filing system for receipts and invoices, and select accounting software that meets your business's needs.

Keeping Track of Events In this part, we will dig into the quick and dirty of keeping exchanges in your books. We'll cover the twofold section bookkeeping framework, which is the groundwork of exact accounting, and clear up how for record different sorts of exchanges, including deals, buys, costs, and finance. Also, we'll talk about the significance of accommodating bank articulations and keeping up with exact records of records payable and records receivable.

Managing Flows of Cash Income the executives is basic for the monetary soundness of your LLC. In this section, we'll investigate techniques for observing and enhancing income, including making income projections, overseeing money due and creditor liabilities, and carrying out powerful invoicing and installment assortment processes. Additionally, we'll talk about the significance of effectively managing working capital and maintaining a cash reserve to cover unexpected expenses.

Financial Analysis and Reporting Monetary revealing gives significant experiences into your LLC's exhibition and monetary position. The income statement, balance sheet, and cash flow statement are the three most important financial statements that every LLC should prepare. In this chapter, we'll talk about them. We'll show you how to interpret these statements to figure out how profitable, liquid, and solvent the company is and where improvements can be made. Furthermore, we'll cover significant monetary proportions and measurements utilized for execution investigation and benchmarking. Charge Consistency for LLCs Charge consistency is a basic part of running an LLC.

The federal, state, and local taxes that are specific to LLCs will be discussed in this chapter. We'll talk about important tax deductions and credits for LLCs, as well as the distinctions between single-member and multi-member LLCs. Also, we'll cover quarterly assessed charge installments, yearly expense filings, and methodologies for limiting duty risk while remaining agreeable with charge laws.Internal Controls and Extortion Avoidance Internal controls are measures put in place to protect the assets of your LLC from fraud.

In this section, we'll examine the significance of carrying out inward controls to alleviate dangers like robbery, misappropriation, and mistakes. We'll investigate best practices for isolation of obligations, approval and endorsement processes, physical and computerized safety efforts, and customary interior reviews. We'll also talk about fraud detection methods and how to deal with suspected fraudulent activity.

Rethinking Accounting Administrations LLCs looking to concentrate on their core business activities may find that outsourcing bookkeeping services is a cost-effective option. In this part, we'll investigate the advantages of reevaluating accounting, including admittance to proficient aptitude, cost reserve funds, versatility, and decreased regulatory weight. We'll talk about how to pick the right accounting specialist organization, arrange administration arrangements, and guarantee information security and privacy.

Development and Extension Procedures Your requirements for bookkeeping may change as your LLC expands. In this chapter, we'll talk about how to upgrade accounting software, add staff or outsource services, and use advanced financial management methods to scale your bookkeeping processes to accommodate growth. We'll likewise investigate the job of accounting in essential navigation, like consolidations and acquisitions, broadening, and global development.

Dominating accounting nuts and bolts is fundamental for the achievement and supportability of your LLC. You can ensure accurate record-keeping, optimize cash flow, comply with tax obligations, and make informed business decisions by understanding the principles of bookkeeping, implementing sound financial practices, and leveraging technology and professional expertise.

You will be well-equipped to navigate the complexities of bookkeeping and position your LLC for long-term growth and success with the knowledge gained from this comprehensive guide.

ºFinancial Statements

Budget reports for Restricted Responsibility Organizations (LLCs) act as essential devices for surveying the monetary wellbeing, execution, and position of these elements. While not as rigid as those for public companies, LLCs actually require exhaustive monetary answering to fulfill inner and outer partners, including proprietors, financial backers, banks, and administrative specialists. In this investigation, we dig into the embodiment of fiscal summaries for LLCs, their parts, importance, and the standards directing their readiness.

Getting a handle on LLC financial statements: Budget summaries for

LLCs normally comprise of three essential archives: the asset report, the pay explanation (or benefit and misfortune articulation), and the income proclamation. Each offers a novel point of view on the monetary remainder of the organization.

1. **Monetary record:** The monetary record gives a depiction of the LLC's monetary situation at a particular moment. It describes the assets, liabilities, and owner equity of the business. The company's cash, accounts receivable, inventory, and fixed assets are all included in the category of assets. The company's obligations, such as accounts payable, loans, and accrued expenses, are represented by liabilities. Proprietor's value mirrors the lingering interest in the organization's resources subsequent to deducting liabilities.

2. **Pay Explanation:** The pay explanation subtleties the LLC's monetary exhibition over a particular period, generally month to month, quarterly, or every year. It records the organization's incomes, costs, gains, and misfortunes to decide its total compensation or overall deficit. Incomes contain all pay created from the organization's essential tasks, while costs incorporate the expenses caused to produce income. Gains and misfortunes emerge from non-working exercises, like resource deals or ventures.

3. **Financial Statement:** During a given time period, the cash flow statement records the inflow and outflow of cash and cash equivalents. It sorts incomes into working, effective money

management, and supporting exercises. Working exercises incorporate money exchanges connected with essential business tasks, like deals and installments to providers. Cash flows from the acquisition or disposal of long-term assets are involved in investing activities. Supporting exercises include incomes connected with outside funding and value exchanges, like credits, speculations, and profits.

Meaning of Budget reports for LLCs: Budget summaries assume an urgent part in working with direction and giving straightforwardness to different partners:

1. **Direction:** Proprietors and administrators utilize budget reports to assess the organization's presentation, recognize regions for development, and go with vital choices. Before providing funding or credit, creditors and investors use these statements to evaluate the company's profitability, solvency, and growth potential.

2. **Responsibility and Straightforwardness:** Fiscal reports improve responsibility by giving a straightforward outline of the LLC's monetary exercises. Stakeholders can use them to keep an eye on the company's adherence to internal policies and procedures and compliance with legal and regulatory requirements.

3. **Evaluation of Performance:** The LLC's financial performance over time is evaluated using financial statements as benchmarks. By contrasting current and verifiable information, partners can check the organization's development direction, benefit patterns, and functional productivity.

Principles for Preparing LLC Financial Statements: While getting ready fiscal reports for LLCs, bookkeepers and monetary experts stick to a few standards to guarantee exactness, dependability, and consistency:

1. Sound accounting standards (GAAP): The standardized accounting principles, standards, and procedures for preparing financial statements are outlined in GAAP, which LLCs adhere to. Sticking to GAAP improves likeness, consistency, and validity of monetary data across various elements.

2. Accumulation Premise Bookkeeping: LLCs normally use accumulation premise bookkeeping, where incomes and costs are perceived when acquired or brought about, paying little mind to when money is traded. When compared to cash basis accounting, this method provides a more accurate depiction of the financial performance and position of the business.

3. Materiality: Financial statements concentrate on important information that users might use to make decisions. When deciding which transactions and events to disclose, accountants put materiality first, making sure that significant details are not missed or misrepresented.

4. Consistency: Consistency is pivotal for keeping up with the similarity of fiscal reports over the long run. From one period to the next, accountants adhere to consistent accounting policies and procedures, minimizing fluctuations and facilitating meaningful analysis.

5. Full admission: Budget summaries incorporate all important data fundamental for clients to grasp the organization's monetary position and execution. The company's contingent liabilities and commitments, as well as important accounting policies, assumptions, and estimates, are made public by accountants.

Budget reports are crucial devices for LLCs, giving important experiences into their monetary wellbeing, execution, and position. By introducing an extensive outline of resources, liabilities, incomes, costs, and incomes, these assertions engage partners to settle on informed choices, advance responsibility, and improve straightforwardness. Adherence to bookkeeping standards, for example, GAAP, accumulation premise bookkeeping, materiality, consistency, and complete story guarantees the precision, unwavering quality, and respectability of monetary detailing for LLCs. As the foundation of monetary examination, these assertions empower proprietors, financial backers, lenders, and controllers to evaluate the suitability and supportability of LLCs in the present powerful business scene.

°Tax Reporting and Filing

Due to their adaptability and liability protection, Limited Liability Companies (LLCs) have grown in popularity among business owners. Notwithstanding, similar to any business substance, LLCs have charge revealing and recording commitments that should be stuck to. In order to avoid penalties and comply with tax laws, LLC owners must be aware of these obligations. We will discuss the intricacies of LLC tax reporting and filing in this comprehensive guide, including tax classifications and annual reporting requirements.

Classification of LLCs in Taxes: The flexibility with which LLCs can be taxed is one of their special characteristics. Naturally, a solitary part LLC is treated as a dismissed substance for charge purposes, implying that the IRS ignores the element, and the proprietor reports business pay and costs on their own government form utilizing Timetable C. Alternately, by submitting Form 8832, Entity Classification Election, an LLC can choose to be taxed as a corporation. The default tax classification for multi-member LLCs is partnership. Similar to single-member LLCs, partnerships do not pay taxes directly; rather, profits and losses are distributed to each member, who reports their share on their own tax returns.Nonetheless, LLCs can likewise choose to be burdened as a partnership whenever wanted.

Charge Revealing Prerequisites for Single-Part LLCs: As referenced before, single-part LLCs are ignored elements for charge purposes, implying that the proprietor reports business pay and costs on their own expense form. This regularly includes recording Timetable C (Structure 1040), Benefit or Misfortune from Business, alongside the proprietor's singular assessment form. Depending on their particular circumstances, single-member LLC owners may be required to file additional tax forms in addition to Schedule C. For instance, if the LLC has employees, the owner must file employment tax forms like Form W-2, Wage and Tax Statement, and Form 941, Employer's Quarterly Federal Tax Return.

Requirements for Multi-Member LLCs' Tax Reporting: The tax reporting requirements for multi-member LLCs are slightly different from those for single-member LLCs, which are taxed as partnerships by default. Each LLC member receives a Schedule K-1 (Form 1065) detailing their share of the LLC's profits, losses, deductions, and credits instead of filing Schedule C. Individuals then, at that point, utilize this data to report their portion of the LLC's pay or misfortune on their singular government forms. As well as giving Timetable K-1 to every part, multi-part LLCs are likewise expected to record a yearly organization assessment form utilizing Structure 1065, U.S. Income from the Partnership Return. This structure sums up the LLC's monetary exercises for the year, including pay, allowances, and credits.

Charge Recording Cutoff times: The IRS and state taxing authorities impose a variety of tax filing deadlines on LLCs, regardless of their tax classification. Unless an extension is requested, the tax filing deadline for single-member LLCs that are taxed as disregarded entities is typically April 15. For multi-part LLCs burdened as organizations, the recording cutoff time for Structure 1065 is the fifteenth day of the third month following the finish of the LLC's fiscal year. For instance, assuming that the LLC's fiscal year closes on

December 31st, the recording cutoff time would be Walk fifteenth. However, LLCs have the same right to request an extension of time to file as individual taxpayers.

Yearly Detailing Prerequisites: LLCs may also be required to report annually in addition to filing taxes by the states in which they are registered. These necessities shift contingent upon the state and may incorporate recording a yearly report or covering establishment charges. Penalties, loss of good standing, and even the LLC's involuntary dissolution can all result from noncompliance with annual reporting requirements. Subsequently, it is fundamental for LLC proprietors to remain informed about their state's announcing necessities and guarantee convenient consistency.

Documentation and Recordkeeping: Legitimate recordkeeping is basic for LLCs to prove their pay, costs, and other monetary exchanges. LLC proprietors ought to keep up with exact and coordinated records, including bank articulations, receipts, solicitations, contracts, and some other pertinent documentation. Notwithstanding monetary records, LLCs ought to likewise hold duplicates of all duty filings, correspondence with charge specialists, and some other archives connected with their assessment revealing and documenting commitments. These records ought to be saved for a predefined period, regularly three to seven years, as they might be mentioned in case of an IRS review or state charge assessment.

Charge detailing and petitioning for LLCs include exploring a perplexing arrangement of rules and guidelines, yet with legitimate comprehension and persistence, LLC proprietors can satisfy their commitments and guarantee consistent with the expense regulations. To avoid penalties and legal consequences, it is essential for any LLC, single or multi member, to accurately report income, timely file tax returns, and keep proper records. By remaining informed and looking for proficient direction when required, LLC proprietors can explore the assessment scene with certainty and spotlight on developing their organizations.

°Real Estate Investing with an LLC

Land effective financial planning offers plenty of chances for abundance gathering and resource expansion. Investing in real estate through the use of a Limited Liability Company (LLC) is a well-liked strategy. This business structure gives various benefits and insurances to financial backers, permitting them to relieve gambles and improve charge productivity while building a vigorous land portfolio.

Advantages of Involving a LLC for Land Effective financial planning:

Security from Liability: One of the essential reasons financial backers decide to contribute through an LLC is the obligation assurance it manages. By laying out a LLC, financial backers can safeguard their own resources from possible claims or claims connected with the properties possessed by the organization. The investor's wealth is protected in the event of unanticipated events like tenant disputes, property damage, or legal obligations by separating personal and business assets.

Flexibility in taxes: LLCs offer extensive adaptability concerning tax assessment, permitting financial backers to pick how they maintain that their business should be burdened. A single-member LLC is treated as a disregarded entity for tax purposes by default, which means that the owner's personal tax return receives the profits and losses. The default tax classification for multi-member LLCs is partnership. Nonetheless, LLCs can likewise choose to be burdened as an enterprise, giving potential advantages, for example, lower charge rates and upgraded derivations.

Security of Assets: Notwithstanding obligation insurance, a LLC can offer resource assurance by compartmentalizing interests into isolated substances. This really intends that assuming one property inside the LLC brings about liabilities or monetary misfortunes, it is doubtful to influence different properties or resources possessed by the financial backer. This division can assist with alleviating dangers and safeguard the general worth of the financial backer's land portfolio.

Functional Adaptability: LLCs give financial backers functional adaptability, permitting them to structure their business in a way that best suits their speculation objectives and inclinations. Financial backers can undoubtedly add or eliminate individuals, dispense benefits and misfortunes, and go with key choices in regards to property procurement, the executives, and demeanor. Investors are able to adjust to shifting market conditions and improve their real estate investment strategies over time thanks to this agility.

Strategies for Using an LLC to Invest in Real Estate:

Security of Assets: Use the restricted obligation insurance of an LLC to defend individual resources from potential dangers related with land speculations. Appropriately organizing the LLC and sticking to lawful conventions can assist with augmenting resource insurance and limit openness to responsibility.

Tax Efficiency: Take advantage of an LLC's tax flexibility to get the most out of your tax return and save money. Talk with charge experts to investigate different expense procedures, like devaluation allowances, 1031 trades, and capital increases arranging, to limit charge liabilities and upgrade generally speaking benefit.

Diversification: Diversify your real estate investments across a variety of property types, locations, and market segments by making use of an LLC's adaptability. Enhancement can assist with relieving gambles related with individual properties or market vacillations, accordingly improving the security and versatility of the venture portfolio.

Management of Professionals: Consider employing professional property management services to manage the LLC's investment properties' day-to-day operations and upkeep. Tasks related to property management can be outsourced, which has the potential to enhance investment returns, tenant satisfaction, and operational efficiencies.

Contemplations While Effective financial planning with a LLC:

Compliance with Law and Regulation: Guarantee consistency with every material regulation, guidelines, and permitting prerequisites administering land speculations and business activities. Inability to stick to legitimate commitments can uncover the LLC and its individuals to possible liabilities and punishments.

Contract of Operation: Draft an exhaustive working understanding illustrating the freedoms, obligations, and dynamic cycles of LLC individuals. The working arrangement ought to resolve main points of contention, for example, benefit sharing, the executives structure, debate goal, and leave systems to stay away from clashes and misconceptions later on.

Tax Repercussions: Look for direction from charge experts or monetary counsels to comprehend the duty ramifications of land ventures led through a LLC. Consider factors, for example, personal duty, independent work charge, capital additions assessment, and devaluation allowances while assessing the general expense productivity of the speculation system.

Management of risk: Property insurance, liability coverage, and contingency planning are all risk management strategies that can be used to reduce potential risks associated with real estate investments. Consistently survey and screen the monetary presentation and market elements of speculation properties to proactively distinguish and address arising chances.

There are numerous advantages to investing in real estate through an LLC, such as liability protection, tax flexibility, asset protection, and operational flexibility. By utilizing the upsides of an LLC structure, financial backers can streamline their land speculation systems, limit dangers, and improve long haul abundance collection. Notwithstanding, it is fundamental to consider legitimate, charge, and functional factors and look for proficient direction to guarantee consistency and boost the possible advantages of effective financial planning with an LLC. With cautious preparation and reasonable independent direction, land financial backers can use the influence of LLCs to construct a strong and enhanced portfolio that creates manageable returns and jelly abundance for people in the future.

CHAPTER 6 ADVANTAGES OF USING AN LLC FOR

REAL ESTATE

In the domain of land speculation, picking the right lawful construction is foremost to safeguarding resources, limiting liabilities, and advancing duty productivity. One famous choice for land financial backers is the Restricted Risk Organization (LLC). A LLC offers a heap of benefits that make it an alluring vehicle for holding and overseeing land resources. There are numerous and significant advantages to using an LLC for real estate investments, including liability protection and tax flexibility.

Limited Liability Protection: The limited liability protection provided by an LLC for real estate investments is one of the primary benefits. By working land ventures through a LLC, financial backers can protect their own resources from any liabilities emerging from the property. In most cases, in the event of a lawsuit, creditors can only pursue the LLC's assets, not the members' personal assets.

Asset Protection: Real estate investments can be vulnerable to a variety of risks, including environmental issues, tenant lawsuits, and damage to the property. An additional layer of asset protection is provided by holding properties inside an LLC. Regardless of whether one property faces legitimate or monetary difficulties, the resources of different properties held inside a similar LLC are by and large shielded from being utilized to fulfill obligations or decisions.

Pass-Through Taxation: LLCs provide pass-through taxation, in which the business does not have to pay taxes on its own income. All things being equal, benefits and misfortunes "go through" to the singular individuals, who report them on their own expense forms. This expense design can be profitable for land financial backers, as it permits them to stay away from twofold tax collection frequently connected with companies.

Charge Adaptability: One of the critical advantages of involving an LLC for land speculations is the adaptability in charge treatment. The members of an LLC can decide how the company will be taxed. They can choose to be burdened as a sole ownership, association, S enterprise, or even a C partnership, contingent upon their particular duty circumstance and inclinations. Investors can tailor their tax strategy to their income level, deductions, and long-term investment objectives thanks to this adaptability.

The executives Adaptability: Not at all like organizations, which are expected to have a directorate and officials, LLCs offer more prominent adaptability in administration structure. The members of an LLC are free to manage the business on their own or to appoint managers to oversee day-to-day operations. Real estate investors are able to structure the management of their properties in a way that best suits their preferences and expertise thanks to this adaptability.

Simplicity of Development and Upkeep: Framing and keeping a LLC is somewhat clear contrasted with other business elements like companies. The majority of states require the filing of articles of organization and payment of a small filing fee to establish an LLC. Also, LLCs have less continuous consistency prerequisites contrasted with partnerships, causing them an appealing choice for land financial backers who favor straightforwardness and simplicity of organization.

Upgraded Validity: Working land ventures through a LLC can improve believability and amazing skill according to inhabitants, banks, and colleagues. Having a conventional business structure conveys a feeling of dependability and authenticity, which can be useful for drawing in occupants and getting funding for future acquisitions.

Bequest Arranging Advantages: LLCs offer benefits in domain arranging and abundance move. Real estate investors can use limited liability companies (LLCs) to facilitate the seamless transfer of ownership interests to heirs and beneficiaries, thereby avoiding probate and minimizing estate taxes through careful estate planning strategies.

Security Assurance: In specific states, LLCs offer security insurance by permitting financial backers to keep their own data classified. Investors can use the LLC as a shield to maintain privacy and anonymity rather than disclosing individual names and addresses on public documents. This can be advantageous for those who wish to keep their real estate holdings private.

Ownership Structure Flexibility: LLCs have a flexible ownership structure that allows for multiple members with varying levels of investment and involvement. Without being restricted by stringent requirements for corporate governance, this flexibility makes it simpler to attract new investors, raise capital, and allocate profits and losses in accordance with the members' agreements.

There are a number of benefits to using an LLC for real estate investments, including protection from limited liability, tax flexibility, management flexibility, and ease of formation.

By utilizing the advantages of an LLC structure, land financial backers can safeguard their resources, limit charge liabilities, and smooth out activities, at last expanding their profits and long haul progress in the serious housing market.

°Purchasing Property through an LLC

In the domain of land speculation, picking the right lawful construction is vital to safeguarding resources, limiting liabilities, and enhancing charge productivity. The Limited Liability Company (LLC) is one popular choice for real estate investors. A LLC offers a bunch of benefits that make it an alluring vehicle for holding and overseeing land resources. There are numerous and significant advantages to using an LLC for real estate investments, including liability protection and tax flexibility.

Restricted Responsibility Security: One of the essential benefits of shaping an LLC for land ventures is the restricted risk assurance it offers. By working land ventures through a LLC, financial backers can protect their own resources from any liabilities emerging from the property. In case of claims, lenders commonly can seek after the resources held inside the LLC, not the individual resources of the individuals. Resource Insurance: Land ventures can be dependent upon different dangers, for example, property harm, claims from occupants, or ecological issues. Holding properties inside an LLC gives an extra layer of resource assurance. Regardless of whether one property faces legitimate or monetary difficulties, the resources of different properties held inside a similar LLC are by and large safeguarded from being utilized to fulfill obligations or decisions.

Pass-Through Taxation: LLCs provide pass-through taxation, in which the business does not have to pay taxes on its own income. Profits and losses, on the other hand, "pass through" to the members, who report them on their individual tax returns. This expense design can be worthwhile for land financial backers, as it permits them to stay away from twofold tax collection frequently connected with companies.

Charge Adaptability: One of the critical advantages of involving an LLC for land ventures is the adaptability in charge treatment. The members of an LLC can decide how the company will be taxed. They can choose to be burdened as a sole ownership, association, S enterprise, or even a C partnership, contingent upon their particular expense circumstance and inclinations. This adaptability permits financial backers to improve their expense methodology in view of elements, for example, pay level, derivations, and long haul speculation objectives.

Management Flexibility: LLCs offer greater management structure flexibility than corporations, which are required to have a board of directors and officers. The members of an LLC are free to manage the business on their own or to appoint managers to oversee day-to-day operations. This adaptability permits land financial backers to structure the administration of their properties such that best suits their inclinations and aptitude.

Simplicity of Arrangement and Upkeep: Shaping and keeping a LLC is somewhat directly contrasted with other business substances like partnerships. The majority of states require the filing of articles of organization and payment of a small filing fee to establish an LLC. Moreover, LLCs have less continuous consistency prerequisites contrasted with partnerships, causing them an appealing choice for land financial backers who favor effortlessness and simplicity of organization.

Upgraded Believability: Working land ventures through a LLC can improve validity and amazing skill according to inhabitants, moneylenders, and colleagues. Having a conventional business structure conveys a feeling of solidness and authenticity, which can be valuable for drawing in occupants and getting funding for future acquisitions.

Domain Arranging Advantages: LLCs offer benefits in bequest arranging and abundance move. Real estate investors can use limited liability companies

(LLCs) to facilitate the seamless transfer of ownership interests to heirs and beneficiaries, thereby avoiding probate and minimizing estate taxes through careful estate planning strategies.

Security Assurance: In specific states, LLCs offer security by permitting financial backers to keep their own data private. Rather than uncovering individual names and addresses on open records, financial backers can involve the LLC as a safeguard to keep up with security and secrecy, which can be favorable for the people who wish to keep their land property hidden.

Adaptability in Possession Construction: LLCs offer adaptability in proprietorship structure, considering the consideration of different individuals with changing degrees of buy-in and contribution. This adaptability makes it more straightforward to get new financial backers, raise capital, and dispense benefits and misfortunes as indicated by the individuals' arrangements, without being obliged by inflexible corporate administration necessities.

Using an LLC for land ventures offers a large number of benefits, including restricted obligation security, charge adaptability, the board adaptability, and simplicity of development. Real estate investors can maximize their returns and long-term success in the competitive real estate market by utilizing the advantages of an LLC structure to safeguard their assets, reduce tax obligations, and streamline operations.

Managing Real Estate Investments

With opportunities for steady income, capital appreciation, and portfolio diversification, real estate investment is a lucrative means of wealth creation. With regards to overseeing land ventures, using a Restricted Responsibility Organization (LLC) design can give a few benefits as far as obligation security, tax reductions, and functional adaptability. We will explore the intricacies of managing real estate investments for limited liability companies (LLCs) in this comprehensive guide, focusing on key topics like formation, asset acquisition, financing, operations, and exit strategies.

Arrangement of a LLC: The formation of the entity itself is the first step in managing real estate investments for an LLC. The members' personal assets are shielded from potential lawsuits or claims stemming from the property's operations by the limited liability shield provided by an LLC. The development interaction normally includes documenting articles of association with the state, drafting a working understanding illustrating the administration design, freedoms, and obligations of the individuals, and getting a Business Recognizable proof Number (EIN) from the IRS.

Acquisition of Assets: The next step is to locate and acquire suitable real estate assets after the LLC is established. Whether it's private properties, business structures, or land advancement projects, cautious reasonable level of effort is fundamental to evaluate the speculation potential, market elements, and hazard factors related with every property. LLCs enable multiple members to pool their resources and invest in a diverse portfolio of properties by offering flexibility in ownership interest structuring. Furthermore, involving a LLC for resource securing gives charge benefits like pass-through tax assessment, where benefits and misfortunes move through to the singular individuals' assessment forms, possibly decreasing generally speaking duty risk.

Funding Methodologies: A lot of money is needed to manage real estate investments, and LLCs can use a variety of financing options to pay for property purchases and development projects. Customary bank advances, business contracts, confidential value associations, and crowdfunding stages are a portion of the normal wellsprings of support used by LLCs. To ensure that each financing option is compatible with the LLC's investment goals and cash flow projections, it is essential to carefully examine its terms, interest rates, repayment schedules, and collateral requirements.

Managing Operations: To get the most out of the real estate assets and minimize risks, efficient operational management is essential. This includes undertakings like occupant screening and renting, property upkeep and fixes, lease assortment, bookkeeping and monetary revealing, consistency with neighborhood guidelines and drafting regulations, and protection inclusion. Members can streamline decision-making procedures, enhance transparency, and lessen the likelihood of conflicts of interest by putting these operational responsibilities in one place and putting them under the umbrella of the LLC.

Risk Moderation and Resource Security: Land speculation intrinsically implies chances, going from market variances and monetary slumps to legitimate debates and catastrophic events. Dealing with these dangers really requires a thorough gamble relief system, which might incorporate protection inclusion, property reviews, possibility holds, lawful defenses like rent arrangements and obligation waivers, and resource enhancement across various geographic areas and property types. A further layer of asset protection is provided by structuring real estate investments within an LLC, shielding the members' personal assets from potential liabilities related to the property's operations.

Planning and Optimization of Taxes: One of the vital advantages of involving a LLC for land ventures is the adaptability it offers as far as expense arranging and improvement. For tax purposes, LLCs are considered pass-through entities, which means that profits and losses are reported on the tax returns of individual members rather than at the entity level. Members can thus reduce their overall tax burden by deducting operating expenses, mortgage interest, property taxes, depreciation, and mortgage interest from their taxable income. In addition,

LLCs can choose to be taxed as either S corporations or C corporations, depending on their particular financial and tax objectives.

Ways to Get Out: Successful leave systems are fundamental for understanding the greatest profit from venture and opening the worth of land resources held by the LLC. Selling the properties outright, refinancing to get more equity, doing 1031 exchanges to avoid paying capital gains taxes, and changing ownership through inheritance or gifting are all common exit strategies. The decision of leave methodology will rely upon different factors, for example, economic situations, venture execution, liquidity needs, and long haul goals of the LLC individuals. To ensure a smooth transition and maximize the financial outcomes for all parties involved, proper planning and execution are essential.

Overseeing land ventures for LLCs requires cautious preparation, execution, and progressing oversight to amplify returns and moderate dangers successfully. Investors can construct a robust portfolio of real estate assets while safeguarding their personal wealth from potential liabilities by utilizing the advantages of limited liability protection, tax advantages, and operational flexibility provided by LLCs. With the right procedures set up, land ventures can act as a solid wellspring of automated revenue, long haul development, and abundance conservation for LLC individuals.

°Protecting Assets and Liabilities

Safeguarding resources and liabilities is a pivotal part of individual and business finance the board. Liabilities are debts or obligations that are owed to other people or entities, whereas assets are valuable possessions or resources owned by individuals or entities. Legitimate security of these resources and liabilities implies a blend of chance administration techniques, lawful structures, and monetary wanting to relieve possible misfortunes and guarantee long haul dependability. Resource insurance envelops different measures pointed toward protecting abundance and assets from likely dangers, including legitimate cases, banks, claims, and monetary slumps. Diversification, which reduces risk exposure by spreading investments across various asset classes like stocks, bonds, real estate, and commodities, is one of the fundamental principles of asset protection. Enhancement limits the effect of market instability and explicit resource class slumps on generally speaking abundance.

Additionally, asset protection entails shielding assets from potential liabilities through the use of legal structures and instruments. In the event of a lawsuit or financial crisis, establishing trusts, limited liability companies (LLCs), and other business entities, for instance, can provide a layer of separation between personal and business assets, limiting the extent to which creditors can access them. In particular, trusts provide protection against estate taxes and probate proceedings while also providing flexibility and control over asset distribution.

By transferring the risk of financial loss to an insurance company in exchange for premium payments, insurance plays a crucial role in asset protection. People and organizations can buy different kinds of insurance contracts customized to their particular necessities, including medical coverage, disaster protection, property protection, and risk protection. In the event of unforeseen circumstances like accidents, illnesses, natural disasters, or legal claims, these policies offer financial compensation or coverage. In addition, asset protection entails putting into action efficient strategies for estate planning in order to guarantee the smooth transfer of wealth to subsequent generations while minimizing tax obligations and legal disputes.

Bequest arranging apparatuses like wills, trusts, legal authorities, and advance mandates empower people to frame their desires with respect to resource dissemination, medical care choices, and guardianship game plans in case of insufficiency or passing. Individuals can safeguard their assets and ensure that their intended beneficiaries receive their inheritance in accordance with their wishes by proactively addressing these issues. To avoid financial distress and maintain financial stability, individuals and businesses must effectively manage liabilities in addition to protecting assets. Liabilities can emerge from different sources, including advances, contracts, Visa obligation, authoritative commitments, and lawful liabilities. Overseeing liabilities implies evaluating gambles, arranging ideal terms, and executing techniques to reimburse obligations as quickly as possibly.

One of the vital standards of risk for the executives is obligation to the board, which includes assessing getting needs, picking proper funding choices, and keeping a good overall arrangement among obligation and value. Inordinate obligation can strain income, increment interest expenses, and block long haul monetary objectives, while too little obligation can restrict potential learning experiences and admittance to capital. As a result, it's critical to strike a balance and only take on debt that can comfortably be serviced and paid back.

Moreover, risk the executives implies distinguishing and relieving potential lawful liabilities that could represent a danger to individual or business resources. This might entail putting in place procedures for risk management, adhering to the requirements for regulatory compliance, and getting the right insurance coverage to guard against lawsuits, claims for negligence, and other kinds of legal disputes. By tending to potential liabilities proactively, people and organizations can limit the gamble of monetary misfortunes and reputational harm.

Powerful gambling of the executives is one more basic part of responsibility insurance, including the distinguishing proof, appraisal, and moderation of potential dangers that could influence monetary security. Risk the board procedures might incorporate expansion of income streams, execution of inner controls and defenses, reception of emergency courses of action, and supporting against explicit dangers through monetary instruments like subsidiaries and insurance contracts.

In addition, keeping up with sufficient liquidity is fundamental for overseeing liabilities and relieving monetary dangers. The capacity to quickly access cash or convert assets into cash without suffering significant losses is referred to as liquidity. Having adequate liquidity guarantees that people and organizations can meet their monetary commitments, reimburse obligations, and cover surprising costs without depending on ablaze deals or resource liquidation at troublesome costs.

Taking everything into account, safeguarding resources and liabilities is fundamental for people and organizations to keep up with monetary soundness, accomplish long haul objectives, and save abundance for people in the future. Individuals and businesses can mitigate potential losses, safeguard against unforeseen risks, and navigate economic uncertainty with confidence by implementing a comprehensive strategy that combines diversification, legal protection, insurance coverage, estate planning, liability management, and risk mitigation strategies. Focusing on resource and obligation insurance isn't just judicious monetary administration yet additionally a key part of getting monetary prosperity and inner serenity.

CHAPTER 7
LIMITED LIABILITY PROTECTION

Restricted obligation security is a key idea in business regulation that assumes an urgent part in molding the cutting edge monetary scene. A legitimate system safeguards entrepreneurs and financial backers from individual risk for the obligations and commitments of the business substance.

This security is principally connected with enterprises and restricted responsibility organizations (LLCs), albeit comparable standards apply to other business designs like associations and sole ownerships in specific purviews. At its center, restricted risk security fills in as a protection for people who put resources into or work organizations. Without this assurance, entrepreneurs would be by and by answerable for every one of the obligations and liabilities caused by the business.

This indicates that the owners' personal assets, such as their homes, savings, and other investments, could be used by creditors to satisfy the business's obligations. Such a situation would stop business ventures and speculation, as people would be reluctant to face the gambling challenges beginning or putting resources into organizations in the event that their own resources were continually in question. As a result, by encouraging entrepreneurship and investment, limited liability protection encourages economic growth and innovation. It lets people take calculated risks without worrying about losing everything they own if a business fails.

This empowers development, as business people are more able to seek after novel thoughts and adventures realizing that their own resources are safeguarded somewhat. One of the critical benefits of restricted obligation assurance is that it takes into account the pooling of capital from different financial backers. In a partnership, for instance, investors can put resources into the organization without being by and by responsible for its obligations. This works with the amassing of assets important for huge scope activities and business tries. Without restricted obligation assurance, financial backers would be reluctant to contribute funding to organizations, seriously restricting their capacity to develop and grow.

Restricted responsibility security additionally advances corporate administration and straightforwardness. Since investors are not actually responsible for the organization's obligations, they are bound to request responsibility and straightforwardness from corporate administration. The company's shareholders and other stakeholders may ultimately gain from improved oversight and decision-making as a result.

Moreover, restricted responsibility security assists with isolating the legitimate character of the business from its proprietors. This idea, known as the "corporate cover," guarantees that the business is treated as a particular lawful substance fit for going into contracts, possessing property, and being sued in its own name. This division of characters gives lucidity and assurance in lawful exchanges and debates, diminishing the gamble of disarray or error. Nonetheless, it is fundamental to perceive that restricted obligation security isn't outright.

There are conditions in which the corporate cover can be penetrated, presenting investors to individual risk. One such situation is when there is proof of misrepresentation or wrongdoing with respect to the proprietors or supervisors of the business. In such cases, courts might dismiss the restricted obligation security and consider people by and by liable for the organization's activities. In addition, shareholders of closely held businesses may occasionally be held personally liable for the debts of the business if they have personally guaranteed the obligations or if the formalities of the business are not followed appropriately.

This features the significance of keeping up with legitimate corporate administration and sticking to lawful prerequisites to save restricted responsibility insurance. The possibility of its misuse or abuse is yet another limitation of limited liability protection. At times, people might endeavor to protect themselves from individual responsibility by taking part in fake or unlawful exercises through a business element. While restricted risk security is expected to energize genuine business exercises, it shouldn't act as a safeguard for unlawful lead.

Courts have the position to puncture the corporate cloak and consider people responsible when there is proof of bad behavior. Lately, there has been a few discussions over the degree of restricted obligation security and its effect on society. Pundits contend that it can prompt moral danger, where people and companies face exorbitant challenges realizing that they won't bear the full results of their activities. This can appear in different structures, like foolish ways of behaving, ecological harm, or monetary wrongdoing.

Pundits likewise highlight situations where organizations default on some loans or participate in resource stripping to abstain from paying banks, passing on partners and networks to endure the worst part of the misfortunes. Regardless of these reactions, restricted risk insurance stays a foundation of present day business regulation and is broadly perceived as a fundamental part of a working business sector economy. It finds some kind of harmony between empowering business and venture while guaranteeing responsibility and straightforwardness in corporate administration.

Limited liability protection fosters economic growth, innovation, and risk-taking by shielding individuals from personal liability for business debts, which ultimately benefits society as a whole. Nonetheless, it is fundamental to maintain the respectability of this legitimate system and address any maltreatments or weaknesses to keep up with its viability and reasonableness.

°Insurance Considerations

In the consistently developing scene of business, Restricted Obligation Organizations (LLCs) have turned into a well known decision among business people because of their adaptable construction and responsibility security. However, LLCs face risks just like any other business entity. LLCs must carefully consider their insurance requirements in order to safeguard their interests and assets. We'll go over important insurance considerations for LLCs, including various insurance types, coverage factors, and risk-management strategies, in this comprehensive guide.

Understanding Restricted Responsibility Organizations (LLCs) Understanding the fundamentals of LLCs is essential prior to delving into insurance considerations. An LLC is a business structure that joins the restricted risk insurance of an enterprise with the adaptability and tax reductions of an association or sole ownership. This construction safeguards the individual resources of LLC individuals (proprietors) from business liabilities, like obligations and claims, while considering go through tax assessment.

Insurance Options for LLCs
Insurance for General Liability: General liability insurance is a necessary protection against third-party claims for bodily injury, damage to property, and advertising harm. For LLCs, this inclusion is fundamental for tending to normal dangers related with everyday tasks, for example, slip-and-fall mishaps, property harm cases, or claims of misleading communication.

Proficient Obligation Protection (Blunders and Oversights Protection): LLCs that offer proficient types of assistance, for example, counseling firms, legitimate practices, or medical services suppliers, ought to think about proficient responsibility protection. Clients could suffer financial losses as a result of claims of negligence, errors, or omissions in the services provided, which are covered by this coverage.

Property Insurance: LLCs that own or lease physical assets like office buildings, equipment, inventory, and furniture need property insurance. This inclusion shields against dangers like fire, robbery, defacing, and catastrophic events, guaranteeing that the LLC can recuperate rapidly from property-related misfortunes.

Laborers' Remuneration Protection: Assuming a LLC has representatives, laborers' pay protection is regularly compulsory in many states. Employees who sustain illnesses or injuries at work are covered by this coverage, which covers costs for treatment, lost wages, and disability benefits. It likewise safeguards the LLC from potential claims emerging from work environment wounds.

Digital Responsibility Protection: In the present computerized age, digital dangers represent a huge gamble to organizations, everything being equal, including LLCs. Digital risk protection mitigates the monetary aftermath from information breaks, cyberattacks, and security infringement by covering costs, for example, criminological examinations, lawful charges, notice expenses, and harms to impacted parties.

Insurance for Directors and Officers (D&O): LLCs with a board of directors or officers should think about buying D&O insurance to shield these individuals from personal liability for the decisions and actions they take on behalf of the business. This inclusion can likewise protect the LLC itself by reimbursing the association for covered misfortunes.

Business Collision protection: On the off chance that a LLC possesses or works vehicles for business purposes, for example, conveyance vans or organization vehicles, business accident coverage is vital. This inclusion gives insurance against mishaps, vehicle harm, and obligation claims coming about because of business-related driving exercises.

What Influences Insurance Coverage? While surveying insurance needs, LLCs ought to consider a few factors that can impact inclusion necessities and payments:

Industry and Business Exercises: The idea of the LLC's activities, industry area, and chance profile will direct the sorts and levels of protection required. High-risk businesses, like development or medical care, may require particular inclusion customized to their particular openings.

Business Size and Income: The size of the LLC, including its yearly income, number of workers, and actual resources, will affect protection needs. Bigger organizations with greater tasks might require higher inclusion cutoff points to safeguard their inclinations enough.

Location: Various risk factors, including weather-related hazards, crime rates, and regulatory environments, can affect the LLC's insurance costs. Organizations working in fiasco inclined regions or thickly populated locales might confront higher charges.

Claims History: The LLC's cases history, including past misfortunes, claims, and insurance claims, can impact back up plans' readiness to give inclusion and the evaluating of payments. While a history of frequent claims may result in higher costs, a favorable claims record may result in lower premiums.

Risk The executives Practices: Proactive gambling the board measures, for example, carrying out security conventions, leading ordinary examinations, and putting resources into representative preparation, can assist with relieving dangers and lower insurance payments. Companies with effective risk management strategies are frequently rewarded by insurers with favorable rates. Systems for Relieving Dangers As well as getting proper protection inclusion, LLCs can embrace different gamble relief procedures to limit possible liabilities and upgrade their general gamble the board system:

Legally binding Assurances: LLCs ought to painstakingly survey and arrange contracts with clients, merchants, and project workers to incorporate repayment statements, limit of risk arrangements, and protection necessities. In business transactions, clear contractual agreements can assist in risk allocation and safeguard the LLC's interests.

Corporate Administration Works on: Keeping up with appropriate corporate administration, including normal executive gatherings, precise record-keeping, and consistency with legitimate and administrative prerequisites, can assist with exhibiting the LLC's obligation to sound strategic approaches and decrease the gamble of lawful debates.

Wellbeing and Consistency Projects: Executing exhaustive security programs, consistency conventions, and quality affirmation measures can limit the probability of mishaps, wounds, and administrative infringement. By focusing on security and consistency, LLCs can moderate functional dangers and upgrade their standing.

Worker Preparing and Schooling: Putting resources into continuous representative preparation and training drives, especially in regions like working environment wellbeing, information security, and moral direct, can engage staff individuals to proactively recognize and address possible dangers. Employees with adequate training are crucial assets for risk management efforts.

Continuous Evaluation and Adjustment: Risk management is an ongoing process that needs to be evaluated and adjusted on a regular basis to deal with new threats, shifting business conditions, and new regulations. LLCs ought to conduct risk assessments on a regular basis and adjust their insurance coverage and risk mitigation strategies in line with those assessments.

Risks, insurance requirements, and risk management strategies must all be carefully considered when navigating LLC insurance considerations. LLCs can enhance their resilience in today's dynamic business environment by understanding the types of insurance that are available, factors that influence coverage, and proactive risk mitigation strategies. LLCs can concentrate on pursuing their objectives, achieving sustainable growth, and mitigating any potential setbacks along the way with the appropriate insurance coverage and risk management strategy.

Asset Protection Strategies

Strategies for protecting personal and business assets from potential risks and liabilities are essential for Limited Liability Companies (LLCs). Members of an LLC receive limited liability protection, shielding their personal assets from lawsuits and business debts. Nonetheless, this security isn't outright, and there are examples where loan bosses or prosecutors can puncture the corporate cover and expect individuals actually to take responsibility. To reduce exposure to such risks, effective asset protection strategies must be implemented. In this thorough aide, we will investigate different resource security methodologies custom fitted for LLCs.

Legitimate Substance Arrangement and Consistency: The groundwork of resource assurance starts with appropriate element development and consistency. This entails meeting all ongoing obligations, such as annual filings and tax compliance, as well as complying with all legal requirements for establishing and maintaining the LLC, such as submitting articles of organization and drafting an operating agreement. It could weaken the LLC's liability protection if its formalities are not followed.

Separation of Personal and Business Assets: For asset protection, it is essential to clearly distinguish between personal and business assets. LLC individuals ought to abstain from blending support by opening separate ledgers for the business, getting a different boss ID number (EIN), and guaranteeing that all exchanges are led for the sake of the LLC as opposed to in their own ability.

Protection Inclusion: Sufficient protection inclusion is a fundamental part of resource assurance. Comprehensive liability insurance policies that are tailored to the risks and industry of an LLC should be purchased. General risk insurance, proficient obligation protection, and umbrella contracts can give extra layers of assurance against claims and claims.

Working Grasping Game plans: The functioning plan is a dire report that approaches the internal capabilities and organization plan of the LLC.

The LLC's defenses against liability may be strengthened by including asset protection provisions in the operating agreement. These provisions may include procedures for handling disputes and liabilities, indemnification clauses, and limitations on member liability.

Using Multiple Limited Liability Companies (LLCs) to Separate Assets: For businesses with a variety of assets or operating divisions, using multiple LLCs to separate assets and shield them from liabilities tied to specific activities is an effective strategy. Limiting risk exposure, each LLC can own and operate its own business unit or asset. The "umbrella LLC" or "Series LLC" strategy allows for risk compartmentalization while maintaining centralized management.

Charging Order Protection: Most states provide LLCs with charging order protection, which prevents creditors from seizing the underlying assets by obtaining a charging order against a debtor-member's distributional interest in the LLC. LLCs can protect assets from direct seizure while maintaining business continuity by restricting creditors' remedies to charging orders.

Resource Assurance Trusts: Resource security trusts, especially homegrown resource insurance trusts (DAPTs) laid out in select states, can supplement LLC structures by giving an extra layer of security for individual resources. DAPTs permit people to move resources into an unavoidable trust, protecting them from leaders' cases after a predetermined time frame has passed.

Family Limited Partnerships (FLPs): When used in conjunction with an LLC, a family limited partnership (FLP) can provide enhanced benefits for asset protection and estate planning. By moving resources for a FLP, people can hold control as broad accomplices while giving restricted organization interests to relatives, subsequently decreasing bequest charge openness and safeguarding resources from leaders.

Homestead Exemption: In states with strong homestead protection, using homestead exemptions can protect individual residences from creditors' claims. LLC individuals can boost this security by appropriately naming their homes and benefiting themselves of any relevant exclusions under state regulation.

Unfamiliar Resource Security Designs: For people with significant resources or global openness, laying out unfamiliar resource assurance structures in purviews with ideal regulations can give extra protection against homegrown loan bosses. Seaward trusts, partnerships, and LLCs can offer security, resource enhancement, and legitimate assurances not accessible locally. Asset protection strategies ought to be evaluated and revised on an annual basis to keep up with shifting legal frameworks, business practices, and personal circumstances. Leading a yearly audit with legitimate and monetary consultants guarantees that resource assurance plans stay compelling and lined up with advancing goals.

Resource security for LLCs is a diverse undertaking that requires cautious preparation, determined execution, and continuous upkeep. By taking on a thorough methodology that consolidates legitimate, monetary, and functional contemplations, LLCs can really safeguard their resources from likely dangers and liabilities, protecting riches and guaranteeing long haul success for their individuals. However, in order to tailor asset protection strategies to the particular requirements and circumstances of each LLC, it is essential to seek advice from qualified professionals, such as attorneys and financial advisors.

°Dissolution and Exit Strategies

As a business structure that is both adaptable and secure, limited liability companies (LLCs) have gained popularity because they provide members with liability protection while allowing for a variety of management structures and tax treatments. In any case, similar to any business substance, an LLC might arrive where disintegration becomes important. Disintegration can happen because of multiple factors, including the normal finish of the business' life expectancy, conflicts among individuals, monetary challenges, or just an adjustment of the individuals' objectives. A well-thought-out exit strategy is essential in these situations to ensure a smooth transition and minimize conflicts.

Grasping Disintegration: The formal procedure of winding up an LLC's affairs and ceasing its operations is referred to as "dissolution." It involves paying off the debts it owes, distributing its assets to creditors and members, and, in the end, ending the company's legal existence. The interaction normally starts with a choice made by the LLC's individuals or as expected by the working understanding or state regulation.

Key Stages in Disintegration:

Part Vote or Understanding: Generally speaking, disintegration requires a vote among the LLC's individuals. Consistent assent is in many cases liked, however the working understanding might determine an alternate edge. Assuming the working arrangement frames disintegration systems, individuals should stick to those arrangements.

Documenting Articles of Disintegration: When the choice to break down is made, the LLC should record articles of disintegration with the state in which it is enlisted. This archive authoritatively informs the express that the LLC is stopping its tasks.

Settling Obligations and Commitments: Prior to appropriating resources for individuals, the LLC should settle its extraordinary obligations and commitments. After creditors have been paid, any assets that remain can be distributed to members based on their ownership interests.

Resource Dissemination: Subsequent to fulfilling lenders' cases, the LLC disperses remaining resources for its individuals. The assignment normally follows the terms illustrated in the working arrangement, which might consider capital commitments, benefit sharing arrangements, or different variables.

Charge Filings and Consistency: All through the disintegration cycle, the LLC should satisfy its duty commitments, including documenting last expense forms and tending to any remaining assessment liabilities. Consistence with state and government charge regulations is urgent to keep away from punishments or legitimate issues.

Methods for Members to Leave: Individual members may also seek to exit the business for a variety of reasons, including retirement, disagreement with other members, or pursuit of other opportunities, in addition to the dissolution of the LLC as a whole. Effective exit strategies can aid members in easing these transitions, safeguarding their interests and minimizing business disruptions.

Buy-Sell Agreements: Buy-sell agreements define the conditions under which a member's interest in the LLC can be sold or transferred. These arrangements frequently address valuation strategies, subsidizing instruments, and limitations on moves to guarantee a systematic change of possession.

Cross-Buy Arrangements: In a cross-buy understanding, every part consents to buy the withdrawing part's advantage in the LLC. While allowing the remaining members to keep control and ensure continuity within the business, this arrangement can provide liquidity for the departing member.

Redemption Agreements: Redemption agreements give the LLC the ability to use company funds to repurchase the interest of a departing member. If the LLC has access to financing or sufficient cash reserves, this strategy may be advantageous, facilitating an easy exit without the need for outside buyers.

Drag-Along and Tag-Along Freedoms: These privileges, frequently remembered for working arrangements, safeguard individuals' inclinations in case of a deal or consolidation of the LLC. Tag-along rights allow minority members to join a sale on the same terms as the majority members, whereas drag-along rights allow majority members to force minority members to participate.

Conveyance of Resources: In the event that is allowed by the working understanding and state regulation, a party might decide to pull out from the LLC and get a relative portion of its resources. However, if the LLC lacks sufficient liquidity or if other members oppose the distribution, this strategy may not be possible.

Tips for Creating a Successful Exit Strategy:

Correspondence and Straightforwardness: Open correspondence among individuals is basic while executing exit methodologies. Misunderstandings and disagreements can be lessened by having open and honest discussions about objectives, expectations, and valuation strategies.

Guidance from a Legal and Financial Professional: Consulting a professional with expertise in LLC law and business transactions can provide valuable insights and ensure compliance with relevant regulations.

Agreements: All exit plans should be written down, preferably in the LLC's operating agreement or in separate agreements. These records ought to frame the agreements of the exit, including valuation strategies, installment terms, and any limitations on moves.

Planning for the Unexpected: In the event of unforeseen circumstances, anticipating potential difficulties and incorporating contingency plans into exit strategies can help reduce risks and ensure a smoother transition.

Disintegration and leave systems are basic parts of dealing with an LLC's lifecycle, offering individuals adaptability and insurance as they explore changing conditions and business goals. LLCs can minimize disruptions, safeguard the interests of members, and facilitate successful transitions for all stakeholders by comprehending the essential steps of dissolution and implementing efficient exit strategies. To achieve positive outcomes, as with any aspect of business management, careful planning, communication, and adhering to financial and legal best practices are necessary.

CHAPTER 8 REASONS FOR DISSOLUTION

Restricted Responsibility Organizations (LLCs) are a famous business structure because of their adaptability, effortlessness, and risk insurance. However, despite these benefits, an LLC may dissolve for a variety of reasons. From monetary hardships to changes in possession or the executives, the choice to disintegrate an LLC can emerge from various variables. In this article, we will investigate the essential purposes behind the disintegration of LLCs and dive into the ramifications of such choices.

Financial Challenges: Monetary hardships are one of the main sources of LLC disintegration. On the off chance that a LLC can't produce adequate income to cover its costs or support benefit, its individuals might choose to break down the organization to try not to gather further obligations or liabilities. Poor business planning, economic downturns, unexpected expenses, or market shifts that render the business model unsustainable are all factors that contribute to financial difficulties.

Debates Among Individuals: Unseen fits of turmoil and questions among individuals can prompt beyond reconciliation contrasts, making it trying to actually work the LLC. Decision-making, profit distribution, management responsibilities, or the business's direction can become increasingly contentious, eventually leading to the LLC's dissolution. In such cases, individuals might find it more judicious to end the business as opposed to keep working in a combative climate.

Management or ownership change: Changes in possession or the board can altogether affect the security and coherence of a LLC. Assuming that vital individuals or partners choose to leave the organization or sell their possession advantages, it can disturb activities and sabotage the attachment of the association. Additionally, the departure of key individuals may result in a loss of knowledge, connections, or resources essential to the LLC's success, leading the remaining members to contemplate dissolution.

Lawful Consistence Issues: An LLC may be subject to a variety of risks, including legal liabilities and fines, if it fails to comply with legal and regulatory requirements. Resistance with charge commitments, authorizing necessities, drafting guidelines, or corporate customs can risk the LLC's capacity to work legitimately and keep up with its lawful standing. In outrageous cases, tireless legitimate difficulties or infringement might propel the individuals to break up the LLC to moderate further lawful openness or unfavorable outcomes.

Achieved Business Objective: Some of the time, an LLC is laid out for a particular reason or task, and when that goal is achieved, there might not be a great explanation to proceed with its presence. For instance, a land improvement LLC shaped to finish a specific development venture might break up upon the undertaker's culmination and the offer of the property. In such cases, the LLC fills its planned need, and disintegration turns into a characteristic movement.

Changes in the market or external factors: Outside factors unchangeable as far as the LLC might be concerned, like changes in shopper inclinations, mechanical progressions, administrative changes, or unexpected market disturbances, can require a reassessment of the business reasonability. It may become impractical or unfeasible to continue operations, prompting the members to choose dissolution, if the LLC's products or services become obsolete, demand declines significantly, or the competitive landscape undergoes significant shifts.

Inability to Obtain Investment or Financing: Restricted admittance to capital or venture subsidizing can upset an LLC's development prospects and cut off its capacity to extend or advance.

Assuming the LLC battles to get support from banks or draw in speculation from expected accomplices or financial backers, it might confront difficulties in subsidizing its activities, satisfying its development targets, or enduring monetary misfortunes. In such cases, the individuals might presume that disintegration is the most reasonable game-plan.

Key Members Died or Were Hurt: The LLC may experience significant operational disruptions and uncertainty as a result of key members' sudden death, incapacity, or death, such as managing partners or majority owners. Without clear progression plans or possibility estimates set up, the excess individuals might find it hard to support the business successfully, driving them to think about disintegration or settling the following difficulties and vulnerabilities.

Diminished Returns or Profitability: Members may be less inclined to continue operating the LLC if there is a decline in profitability, returns on investments, or overall financial performance. Instead of remaining in a business that no longer offers satisfactory returns or growth prospects, its members may choose to dissolve the LLC if it fails to meet its members' expectations or generate sufficient profits.

Vital Rebuilding or Revamping: Vital rebuilding or redesign drives, for example, consolidations, acquisitions, side projects, or divestitures, may provoke the disintegration of a LLC as a component of a more extensive corporate system. In the event that the

LLC's resources, tasks, or market position can be better enhanced or utilized through coordination with another substance or through an alternate corporate design, disintegration might be considered significant to work with the change and acknowledge vital goals.

The choice to break down an LLC can originate from different elements, including monetary difficulties, unseen struggles, changes in proprietorship or the executives, legitimate consistency issues, accomplishment of business targets, market elements, supporting limitations, key staff changes, declining productivity, or key goals. In the explanation, LLC disintegration addresses a critical choice that requires cautious thought of the ramifications and ramifications for all partners included. By figuring out the normal explanations behind disintegration and resolving hidden issues proactively, LLC individuals can pursue informed choices that serve their wellbeing and safeguard the worth made by the business.

ºWinding Up Business Affairs

Restricted Risk Organizations (LLCs) offer entrepreneurs adaptability, obligation assurance, and expense benefits. Nonetheless, every undertaking in the long run reaches a conclusion. Whether because of key choices, monetary difficulties, or changes in private conditions, ending up a LLC is an urgent cycle that requires cautious thought and adherence to legitimate commitments. The intricacies of winding up LLC business affairs will be discussed in detail in this guide, including the necessary steps, legal requirements, and best practices to ensure a smooth transition.

Understanding the End: The systematic process of liquidating assets, paying off debts, and distributing any remaining funds or assets to members is required to wind up an LLC. It signifies the business entity's dissolution and formal conclusion to its operations. While the particular advances might shift relying upon state regulations and the LLC's working understanding, there are crucial rules that apply all around.

Starting the Wrapping Up Cycle: The choice to end up a LLC might emerge from different conditions, including the lapse of the LLC's expression, accomplishment of its motivation, or a partial vote to break up. The process typically begins with a formal resolution or unanimous consent from all members to dissolve the LLC, regardless of the reason. This goal ought to be archived and kept up with for lawful purposes.

Compliance and notification: When the choice to wrap up has been made, the LLC should inform applicable partners, including leaders, providers, and government organizations. The LLC must frequently file dissolution paperwork with the Secretary of State or publish a notice of dissolution in local newspapers in accordance with state law. Consistency with charge commitments, including recording last assessment forms and settling any remaining duty liabilities, is fundamental to stay away from punishments or lawful repercussions.

Asset liquidation and debt settlement: Liquidation includes changing over the LLC's resources into cash or attractive protections to work with obligation reimbursement and dissemination to individuals. Selling both intangible assets like intellectual property rights and investments, as well as tangible assets like equipment or inventory, may be part of this procedure. Continues from resource deals are utilized to settle remarkable obligations, including advances, leases, and authoritative commitments. Focusing on loan boss cases and following legal methods for obligation reimbursement is basic to stay away from possible lawful questions.

Dissolution and Distribution of Members: Any assets that are left over are divided among LLC members in accordance with their ownership interests, as outlined in the operating agreement, after all debts have been paid off. The distribution procedure is typically governed by state laws in the absence of specific provisions. It's essential to record the circulation of resources and acquire waivers or deliveries from individuals affirming their receipt of their portion of the LLC's resources. To officially end its existence, the LLC must submit articles of dissolution or another document of a similar nature to the Secretary of State.

Legitimate Contemplations and Obligation Assurance: All through the wrapping up process, LLC individuals should stick to lawful prerequisites and satisfy trustee obligations to leaders and individual individuals. Inability to do so could bring about private obligation openness or legitimate difficulties. Looking for proficient direction from lawyers or monetary counselors experienced in business disintegration can assist alleviate gambles and guarantee consistency with relevant regulations.

Obligations Following the Divorce: Certain obligations, such as winding up the LLC's final business affairs, settling any remaining claims or disputes, and filing additional tax returns or reports as required by federal or state authorities, may continue even after the LLC has been officially dissolved. Keeping up with exact records and documentation of the disintegration cycle is vital to address any expected difficulties or requests that might emerge from now on.

Wrapping up business undertakings for LLCs is a multi-layered process that requires cautious preparation, adherence to lawful prerequisites, and viable correspondence among partners. Members of an LLC can successfully navigate the winding up process and conclude their business endeavors on a positive note by complying with legal requirements, understanding the steps involved, and seeking professional guidance when necessary. While the choice to break down a LLC might check the finish of one part, it additionally makes ready for new open doors and attempts from now on.

°Closing an LLC

Shutting a LLC (Restricted Obligation Organization) denotes the finish of a business substance's excursion. Whether because of an adjustment of conditions, monetary reasons, or key choices, the method involved with shutting a LLC is a huge step that requires cautious regard for legitimate, monetary, and managerial subtleties. The intricacies of dissolving an LLC, from the initial considerations to the final steps, will be examined in depth in this guide.

Section 1: Beginning Contemplations
Shutting a LLC isn't a choice to be trifled with. It includes lawful commitments, monetary ramifications, and likely ramifications for partners. Prior to starting the disintegration cycle, LLC proprietors ought to think about the accompanying:

Explanations behind Conclusion: Figure out the inspirations driving shutting the LLC. It may very well be because of monetary challenges, changes in private conditions, absence of productivity, or vital changes in the business center.

Legal Requirements: Examine the LLC's operating agreement and state dissolution laws. Guarantee consistency with the particular necessities illustrated in these reports.

Monetary Appraisal: Evaluate the LLC's monetary standing, including obligations, resources, and remarkable commitments. Foster an arrangement to settle obligations and circulate remaining resources among individuals.

Correspondence with Partners: Illuminate pertinent gatherings, including co-proprietors, representatives, loan bosses, and clients, about the choice to close the LLC. Straightforwardness and open correspondence can assist with overseeing assumptions and relieve possible contentions.

Section 2: Disintegration Interaction When the choice to close the LLC is made, the disintegration interaction can start. For the business to be officially dissolved, this requires several steps. The specific requirements for an LLC may differ from state to state, but they typically include the following:

Vote to Break up: Hold a gathering of LLC individuals to decide on the choice to disintegrate the organization. Regarding the required majority vote, adhere to the procedures outlined in the operating agreement and state laws.

Document Articles of Disintegration: Plan and record articles of disintegration with the state government organization liable for business filings. The LLC's intention to dissolve is officially announced in this document to the state.

Settle Obligations and Commitments: Sell resources, settle exceptional obligations, and satisfy any legally binding commitments. This might include selling resources, taking care of lenders, and ending leases or agreements.

Inform Loan bosses and Expense Specialists: Give composed notice of the LLC's disintegration to lenders, providers, and other pertinent gatherings. Likewise, illuminate government, state, and neighborhood charge specialists about the conclusion of the business.

Drop Licenses and Allows: Drop any permits to operate, grants, or enlistments held by the LLC. This guarantees that the organization is presently not at risk for reestablishment charges or administrative commitments.

Section 3: Circulation of Resources The LLC's remaining assets can be divided among members based on their ownership interests once debts and obligations are settled.

The following steps are typically included in this procedure:

Stock Resources: Gather an extensive rundown of the LLC's excess resources, including cash, stock, hardware, protected innovation, and some other property claimed by the organization.

Valuation of Assets: To ensure an equitable distribution among members, determine the fair market value of each asset. Consider recruiting an expert appraiser for mind boggling or high-esteem resources.

Adopt a Distribution Plan: Members of an LLC should come to an agreement on a distribution plan that outlines how the remaining assets will be divided between them. This may be determined by agreed-upon ownership percentages or other criteria.

Execute Distribution: As per the agreed-upon plan, transfer ownership of assets to individual members. Guarantee legitimate documentation, including bills of offer, task arrangements, and move reports. Section

4: Expense Contemplations Shutting a LLC has critical expense suggestions for both the business substance and its individuals. It is fundamental to comprehend these ramifications and find fitting ways to satisfy charge commitments.

Important factors include: Last Government forms: Document last administrative, state, and neighborhood expense forms for the LLC. This includes employment tax returns, income tax returns, and any other filings that are required for the tax year in which the marriage ends.

Charge Freedom Testament: A few states require LLCs to get a duty leeway endorsement or comparable documentation from charge specialists prior to settling the disintegration interaction. This demonstrates that all owed taxes have been paid.

Pass-Through Taxation: On their individual tax returns, LLC members may be responsible for reporting their share of the LLC's income, gains, losses, and deductions. Talk with an expense guide to guarantee consistency with pertinent duty regulations.

Capital Gains Tax: LLC members may be subject to capital gains tax on any profits generated by the dissolution, depending on the nature of asset sales or distributions. Plan as needed is to limit charge liabilities. Section

5: Last Regulatory Advances To close an LLC and ensure compliance with legal requirements, various administrative tasks must be completed.

The following are some final considerations:

Drop Business Enlistments: Inform state and nearby specialists, as well as applicable industry administrative bodies, of the LLC's conclusion. Drop any business enlistments, allows, or licenses held by the organization.

Advise Specialist co-ops: Illuminate specialist organizations, like utilities, protection suppliers, and landowners, of the LLC's disintegration. Close records, end agreements, and settle any remaining adjusts.

Worker Matters: In the event that the LLC has representatives, conform to government and state regulations in regards to representative end, including last checks, benefits continuation, and warning of joblessness protection qualification.

Recordkeeping: Keep up with nitty gritty records of the disintegration interaction, including meeting minutes, monetary exchanges, correspondence with partners, and legitimate documentation. Future audits or references may require these records.

The process of closing an LLC is complicated and necessitates careful preparation, execution, and adherence to legal and regulatory requirements. By following the means illustrated in this aid and looking for proficient counsel when important, LLC proprietors can explore the disintegration cycle effectively and limit likely dangers and liabilities. While shutting a LLC marks the finish of one section, it additionally prepares for new open doors and tries from now on.

°Case Studies and Examples

Restricted Risk Organizations (LLCs) have turned into a famous decision for organizations because of their adaptable design and the obligation security they propose to their proprietors. In this essay, we will look at various examples and case studies that show the benefits and drawbacks of starting and running an LLC.

Contextual investigation 1: **Independent venture Accomplishment with a LLC:**

Background: Sarah and John, two business people, chose to begin a little visual computerization office. They established an LLC with the name "Creative Designs, LLC" because they were concerned about personal liability and desired a flexible business structure.

Advantages of the LLC:

Restricted Responsibility: When the organization confronted a claim because of copyright encroachment, Sarah and John's own resources were safeguarded. Just the resources of the LLC were in danger.

Charge Adaptability: Innovative Plans, LLC selected to be burdened as an organization, permitting them to go through benefits and misfortunes to their own expense forms, staying away from twofold tax collection. Flexibility in management: Sarah and John were able to easily run the business without the formalities of a corporation.

Outcome: In spite of the legitimate test, Imaginative Plans, LLC kept on flourishing. The protection and adaptability their business required to succeed were provided by the LLC structure. Contextual analysis

2: Land Venture:

Background: James, a financial backer, needed to buy a few investment properties to produce automated revenue. He framed an LLC, "Property Adventures, LLC," to hold and deal with his land ventures.

Advantages of the LLC

Resource Security: By holding the properties under the LLC, James safeguarded his own resources from potential claims connected with the properties.

Go through Tax collection: Property Adventures, LLC chose to be burdened as a pass-through substance, permitting James to report benefits and misfortunes on his own expense form.

Simplicity of Move: When James needed to get extra financial backers, the LLC structure considered the simple exchange of proprietorship interests.

Outcome: Property Adventures, LLC empowered James to construct a differentiated land portfolio while moderating individual risk and improving on charge revealing. Contextual investigation

3: Privately-owned company Change

Background: The Smith family possessed a fruitful assembling business. They looked for a structure that would protect their assets and make it easier to plan for the business's future as they got ready to hand it over to the next generation.

Advantages of the LLC: Coherence: By moving possession interests in the LLC to relatives steadily, the Smiths guaranteed a smooth progress of control and the board.

Restricted Responsibility: As the business extended, the LLC protected the family's very own resources from the dangers related with working an assembling office.

Domain Arranging: Through the LLC working arrangement, the Smiths had the option to frame progression plans and cast ballot rights, guaranteeing the business stayed inside the family.

Outcome: The LLC structure permitted the Smith family to keep up with command over their business while planning for the cutting edge to assume control, guaranteeing the coherence and life span of the family undertaking.

Difficulties and Illustrations Learned: Despite the numerous advantages that LLCs provide, business owners must navigate the following obstacles: Intricacy of Development: Setting up a LLC expects adherence to state guidelines and drafting complete working arrangements, which can be perplexing and tedious.

Tax Considerations: Although LLCs provide tax flexibility, owners must carefully consider the tax implications of their chosen structure and consult with tax professionals. Management Structure: LLCs may encounter management disputes that can impede decision-making and expansion if the operating agreement does not clearly define roles and responsibilities.

It is clear from the case studies and examples provided that limited liability companies (LLCs) provide significant advantages to businesses of all sizes and sectors. From little new businesses to laid out ventures, the LLC structure gives obligation assurance, charge adaptability, and the board independence. However, owners of businesses need to be aware of the difficulties that come with setting up and running an LLC, and they should make sure they have the support and guidance they need to succeed. By and large, LLCs stay a famous decision for business people looking to safeguard their resources and improve their business tasks.

CHAPTER 9 SUCCESSFUL LLC VENTURES

Restricted Responsibility Organizations (LLCs) have arisen as a famous decision for business people looking to lay out their endeavors. Offering a mix of responsibility security and adaptability, LLCs have turned into a foundation of the business scene.

Nonetheless, making progress with an LLC adventure requires something other than desk work; it requests key preparation, constancy, and a readiness to adjust. In this investigation, we dive into the subtleties of effective LLC adventures, uncovering the systems, entanglements, and wins en route.

Grasping the Establishment: A solid foundation lies at the heart of every successful LLC venture. The company's vision, mission, and core values form the basis of this foundation. Entrepreneurs must identify how their product or service uniquely meets the needs of their target market, comprehend their customers' requirements, and define their target market. In addition, choosing the right business structure is pivotal. LLCs offer an equilibrium of risk security and adaptability, permitting proprietors to appreciate go through tax collection while safeguarding their own resources from business liabilities. Nonetheless, understanding the lawful and monetary ramifications of framing a LLC is fundamental to stay away from likely traps not too far off.

Techniques for Progress:

Statistical surveying and Approval: A thorough market analysis is essential for any LLC venture. Product development, pricing strategies, and marketing efforts can all benefit from an understanding of market trends, consumer preferences, and competitor strategies. In addition, the risk of entering saturated or unprofitable markets can be reduced by validating the business concept through pilot testing, focus groups, or surveys.

Networks and Strategic Partnerships: Opportunities that might not have been possible on their own may become available by forging strategic alliances and cultivating a robust network. Working together with corresponding organizations, providers, or industry powerhouses can upgrade market reach, believability, and asset access. Organizing through industry occasions, meetings, and online stages can likewise prompt important associations, mentorship, and possible financial backers.

Nimble Variation and Development: Successful LLC ventures are characterized by adaptability and flexibility. In the present powerful business climate, having the option to turn rapidly in light of market changes, mechanical headways, or unexpected difficulties is fundamental. LLCs can aid in staying ahead of the curve and remaining competitive by embracing innovation, experimenting with novel concepts, and continuously improving products or services.

Monetary Administration and Maintainability: Any LLC endeavor depends on effective financial management. Laying out a reasonable spending plan, overseeing income really, and observing key monetary measurements are basic for long haul manageability. In addition, diversifying revenue streams, securing adequate funding, and anticipating unforeseen expenses can protect against economic downturns.

Things to Avoid:

Absence of Arranging and Technique: One of the most widely recognized entanglements for LLC adventures is an absence of thorough preparation and methodology. Neglecting to characterize clear objectives, recognize target showcases, or foster a practical plan of action can prompt erratic execution and squandered assets. Business visionaries should put time and exertion into creating a hearty marketable strategy that frames targets, techniques, and achievements.

Lacking Legitimate and Consistence Getting it: Obliviousness of lawful and consistent necessities can mean ruin for LLC adventures. Contracts and intellectual property rights to registration and taxation, navigating the legal landscape can be difficult and intimidating. Looking for proficient direction from lawyers, bookkeepers, or business counselors is fundamental to guarantee consistency and relieve legitimate dangers.

Unfortunate Authority and Group Elements: Compelling administration and firm group elements are urgent for LLC achievement. Business people should rouse certainty, impart vision, and cultivate a culture of joint effort and responsibility inside their groups. Employee morale and productivity can be improved by hiring the right people, providing ongoing training and support, and encouraging a healthy work-life balance.

Dismissing Promoting and Marking: Without effective branding and marketing, a product or service will struggle to gain traction, regardless of how innovative or high-quality it is. Forgetting to put resources into marking, advanced showcasing, or client securing procedures can bring about haziness and botched open doors. LLC adventures should dispense assets towards building brand mindfulness, drawing in with ideal interest groups, and developing client reliability.

Wins and Achievements:

Accomplishing Item Market Fit: The achievement of product-market fit, or alignment between a product or service and the requirements of its target market, is perhaps one of an LLC venture's most significant victories. This achievement means approval of the business thought, broad reception by clients, and the potential for versatile development.

Expansion and Scaling: Effectively scaling a LLC adventure past its underlying stages is a demonstration of its flexibility and versatility. Whether through geographic extension, enhancement of product offerings, or vital associations, scaling requires cautious preparation, asset portion, and hazard the executives. For the business and its stakeholders, each new milestone in the scaling process is a victory.

Building a Strong Community and Brand: A significant achievement for LLC ventures is cultivating a loyal community of customers, advocates, and employees as well as establishing a strong brand identity. Brands that resonate with their ideal interest group, inspire positive feelings, and represent something significant can order premium evaluation, appreciate supported development, and endure serious tensions.

Impact and value creation: Eventually, the genuine proportion of progress for an LLC adventure lies in the worth it makes for its partners and the effect it has on society. Businesses that put purpose ahead of profit can leave a lasting legacy and inspire others to follow in their footsteps by creating jobs, innovating, giving back to the community, or protecting the environment.

There are difficulties, opportunities, and triumphs along the way to a successful LLC venture. By establishing a strong groundwork, executing powerful techniques, keeping away from normal entanglements, and praising achievements en route, business visionaries can explore the intricacies of business proprietorship with certainty and flexibility. As the business scene keeps on developing, the people who embrace development, versatility, and a promise to greatness will flourish in the steadily evolving commercial center.

ºLessons Learned from Failed Ventures

Especially when starting a Limited Liability Company (LLC), starting a business venture is an exhilarating journey full of promise and potential. However, the truth is that not all endeavors are successful. Disappointment is an inescapable piece of business, yet it additionally offers priceless illustrations. In this discussion, we delve into the essential lessons that LLCs can learn from unsuccessful ventures, highlighting the dangers to avoid and the strategies to implement for future success.

Figuring out Disappointment: Disappointment isn't inseparable from rout; rather, it is a venturing stone to development and illumination. It is essential to carry out a comprehensive post-mortem analysis in order to comprehend the underlying reasons for the failure of an LLC venture. The foundation for valuable lessons that can guide future endeavors is laid by this introspection.

Example 1:
Absence of Statistical surveying: Lack of thorough market research is a major contributor to venture failure. LLCs should carefully investigate market patterns, buyer conduct, and serious scenes prior to sending off an item or administration. Inability to do so can bring about skewed contributions, unfortunate market fit, and at last, decreased request.

Example 2:
Lacking Monetary Administration: Numerous LLCs frequently fail as a result of poor financial management. From overspending on trivial costs to misjudging functional expenses, poor monetary arranging can rapidly prompt bankruptcy. For long-term viability, it is essential to establish a robust financial management system that includes cash flow analysis, forecasting, and budgeting.

The Inability to Pivot: Versatility is vital to endurance in the powerful business scene. In any case, some LLCs neglect to perceive the need to turn in light of changing economic situations or arising patterns. The most important qualities are adaptability and agility, which enables businesses to modify their strategies and offerings to better meet changing customer demands.

Example 4:

Powerless Marking and Showcasing: LLCs need strong branding and marketing to stand out from the competition and attract customers' attention. Inability to lay out a convincing brand personality or execute designated promoting efforts can bring about unfortunate perceivability and dreary deals. Putting resources into proficient marking and advertising procedures is fundamental for developing brand value and driving development.

Lesson 5:

Team Dynamics and Lack of Leadership: Solid initiative and strong group elements are central to the progress of any LLC adventure. Unfortunate initiative, incapable correspondence, and relational contentions can wreck progress and subvert spirit. Developing a positive work culture, cultivating open correspondence, and engaging colleagues are basic for encouraging joint effort and driving achievement.

Illustration 6:

Disregarding Lawful and Consistence Commitments: LLCs should comply with different legitimate and consistent commitments to work inside the limits of the law. Forgetting to satisfy administrative prerequisites, like duty filings, permitting, and contract commitments, can bring about expensive punishments and lawful questions. For risk mitigation and business continuity, it is essential to prioritize legal compliance and seek professional advice when necessary.

Seventh Lesson:

Excessive Reliance on External Funding: While getting outer subsidizing can give vital money to fuel development, overreliance on financing can be adverse. LLCs that neglect to accomplish manageable income streams or become excessively obliged may end up in tricky monetary positions. Finding some kind of harmony between outer subsidizing and natural development is significant for long haul monetary strength.

Illustration 8:

Inability to Gain from Errors: Maybe the most basic example of everything is the significance of gaining from previous oversights. LLCs are doomed to repeat their mistakes if they do not acknowledge and address them. For ongoing success, it is essential to cultivate a culture of continuous improvement, solicit feedback, and translate lessons learned into practical strategies.

Bombed adventures for LLCs offer an abundance of experiences that can illuminate future pioneering tries. LLCs can position themselves for long-term success in a business environment that is becoming increasingly competitive by comprehending the underlying causes of failure and accepting the lessons learned. Each lesson provides a useful pointer on the way to success as an entrepreneur, from market research and financial management to branding and team dynamics.

°Future Trends and Considerations

Due to their adaptability, simplicity, and liability protection, limited liability companies (LLCs) have grown in popularity among business owners. The landscape of LLCs is likely to be shaped by several trends and factors as we look ahead. In this paper, we will investigate what's in store patterns and contemplations that might affect the arrangement, activity, and administration of LLCs.

Increasing Adoption and Popularity: LLCs have encountered consistent development in fame throughout recent many years, and this pattern is probably going to go on from here on out. The effortlessness of development and the adaptability in administration make LLCs an alluring choice for business people and entrepreneurs. It is anticipated that the number of LLCs will rise as more people seek to start businesses or safeguard their assets.

Changes to the law and compliance: Administrative necessities for LLCs might advance in light of changing financial circumstances, cultural assumptions, and government strategies. Future guidelines might zero in on improving straightforwardness, corporate administration, and responsibility inside LLCs. To avoid penalties and legal obligations, LLCs must continue to comply with tax laws, reporting requirements, and industry-specific regulations.

The Integration of Technology: Mechanical headways will keep on influencing how LLCs work and collaborate with partners. Digital platforms and tools will simplify administrative tasks, make communication easier, and make LLCs work more efficiently. The management of ownership, contracts, and transactions within LLCs may be made easier and safer with the help of blockchain technology.

Operations Across Borders and Globalization: As organizations progressively work on a worldwide scale, LLCs might have to explore complex lawful and administrative systems in numerous locales. Worldwide tax collection, economic deals, and social contrasts will impact the construction and activity of LLCs with cross-line tasks. LLCs might investigate associations, joint endeavors, or auxiliaries in unfamiliar business sectors to grow their span and relieve gambles.

Considerations related to governance, society, and the environment (ESG): LLCs' behavior and decision-making will be influenced by investors, customers, and regulators' growing focus on ESG factors. LLCs might integrate supportability rehearses, moral guidelines, and variety drives into their business techniques to line up with ESG assumptions. Inability to address ESG concerns could result in reputational harm, lawful questions, and monetary misfortunes for LLCs.

Lawful and Responsibility Issues: As courts interpret statutes, precedents, and contractual agreements, the legal landscape surrounding LLCs may change. LLCs might confront difficulties connected with penetrating the corporate shroud, part debates, licensed innovation privileges, and information protection concerns. Proactive gambling the board procedures, including protection inclusion and lawful insight, will be fundamental for safeguarding LLCs against possible liabilities.

Elective Plans of action: The ascent of the gig economy, independent work, and cooperative stages might lead to new sorts of LLCs custom fitted to the requirements of self employed entities and solopreneurs. Adaptable enrollment structures, decentralized navigation, and virtual activities could portray these option LLC models. In order to compete with new business models and attract top talent, traditional LLCs may need to modify their policies and structures.

Segment Movements and Generational Inclinations: Evolving socio economics, for example, the maturing populace and the ascent of recent college grads and Age Z, will impact customer inclinations, labor force elements, and business patterns. LLCs might have to oblige assorted viewpoints, values, and ways of life to stay significant and serious in the commercial center. LLCs will need strategies for succession planning, leadership development, and employee engagement to get through generational shifts and keep talent.

As Restricted Responsibility Organizations (LLCs) keep on

developing in light of monetary, mechanical, and social changes, entrepreneurs and partners should stay cautious and versatile. LLCs can position themselves for long-term success in an increasingly complex and interconnected world by remaining informed about future trends and considerations. Whether it's embracing development, agreeing with guidelines, or focusing on supportability, LLCs must proactively address provocations and take advantage of chances to flourish later on the business scene.

CHAPTER 10 EVOLVING REGULATIONS AND LAWS

Due to their adaptable structure and liability protection, Limited Liability Companies (LLCs) have grown in popularity among entrepreneurs and business owners. Be that as it may, exploring the administrative scene encompassing LLCs requires a comprehension of developing regulations and guidelines. This article investigates the unique idea of guidelines and regulations administering LLCs, inspecting key changes and their suggestions.

Authentic Outline of LLC Guidelines: Late in the 1970s, LLCs emerged as a hybrid business structure that combined the advantages of partnerships and corporations. At first, guidelines shifted by state, with few government rules. State regulations fundamentally administered arrangement, the executives, and tax assessment from LLCs.

Advancement of Government Guidelines: The IRS issued Revenue Ruling 88-76 in 1988, which established guidelines for LLC tax classification. The ruling made it clear that LLCs could choose to be taxed like corporations or partnerships, laying the groundwork for federal recognition.

The Ascent of State-Explicit Guidelines: All through the 1990s and mid 2000s, states started authorizing LLC rules, giving complete rules to arrangement, activity, and disintegration. Due to favorable regulations and business-friendly environments, popular choices like Delaware and Wyoming emerged.

Administrative Difficulties in the Advanced Age: LLC regulations faced new difficulties as a result of the proliferation of e-commerce and digital business models. States refreshed regulations to address online activities, electronic marks, and virtual gatherings, mirroring the advancing idea of strategic policies.

Concentrate on Compliance and Corporate Governance: In light of corporate outrages and monetary emergencies, controllers escalated examination on corporate administration and consistency. LLCs confronted expanded detailing necessities, revelation commitments, and straightforwardness norms to forestall misrepresentation and unfortunate behavior.

Effects of International Trade and Globalization: Globalization extended open doors for LLCs to participate in worldwide exchange and cross-line exchanges. frameworks of regulation that have been modified to accommodate foreign investments, export-import regulations, and international standards compliance.

Natural and Social Obligation: LLC regulations included sustainability measures as a result of regulators' growing awareness of social and environmental issues. Green drives, corporate social obligation (CSR), and moral strategic policies became basic parts of consistency for LLCs.

Advances in technology and data privacy: Concerns about consumer privacy and data security were raised by technological advancements, particularly in data collection and analytics. LLC guidelines developed to address information insurance regulations, online protection measures, and consistency with security guidelines like GDPR and CCPA.

Economic Crises and the Response of Regulators: Regulator reforms aimed at bolstering financial institutions and protecting investors were initiated in response to the financial crisis of 2008. LLC guidelines went through corrections to improve security, risk the board, and responsibility in the outcome of financial slumps.

Administrative Patterns and Strategy Movements: Changes in political authority and changes in arrangement needs affected LLC guidelines. The business environment for LLCs was impacted by legislative trends that reflected debates regarding healthcare reform, trade agreements, economic stimulus measures, and tax reform.

Cooperative Administration and Partner Commitment: Controllers progressively underlined cooperative administration and partner commitment to cultivate straightforwardness and responsibility. Public interviews, industry discussions, and administrative sandboxes gave roads to enter from partners, including LLCs and their delegates.

Future Viewpoint and Arising Patterns: Looking forward, the administrative scene for LLCs is supposed to keep advancing because of mechanical advancement, international elements, and cultural changes. LLCs face new regulatory challenges and opportunities from emerging trends like blockchain technology, decentralized finance (DeFi), and artificial intelligence (AI).

Due to historical developments, economic trends, and societal shifts, the regulatory framework for LLCs has undergone significant change over time. As business scenes develop, guidelines administering LLCs will keep on adjusting to address the issues of partners, guarantee consistency, and advance mindful strategic approaches in a steadily evolving climate.

Understanding and exploring these advancing guidelines are fundamental for LLCs to flourish and prevail in the powerful worldwide commercial center.

°Technological Innovations in LLC Management

Restricted Obligation Organizations (LLCs) have for some time been a famous decision for business visionaries and entrepreneurs because of their adaptability, effortlessness, and risk insurance. Managing an LLC, on the other hand, necessitates careful attention to various administrative tasks, regulations, and channels of communication. Solutions to simplify administrative tasks, enhance communication, enhance compliance, and facilitate overall business operations have been provided by technological innovations in LLC management.

Artificial Intelligence and Automation: Robotization and man-made consciousness (simulated intelligence) advancements have reformed LLC the executives via mechanizing dull errands, diminishing human blunder, and further developing effectiveness. Simulated intelligence controlled programming arrangements can mechanize bookkeeping processes, receipt age, finance the executives, and consistency following, saving time for entrepreneurs to zero in on essential navigation and development drives.

Tools for Collaboration in the Cloud: Cloud-based joint effort instruments have changed the manner in which

LLCs deal with their tasks by empowering continuous cooperation, archive sharing, and venturing the executives from anyplace with a web association. Stages like Google Work area, Microsoft 365, and Slack work with consistent correspondence among colleagues, considering productive navigation and task coordination.

Blockchain for Straightforwardness and Security: With its unparalleled transparency, security, and traceability, blockchain technology has revolutionized LLC management. LLCs can automate contract execution, keep track of ownership shifts, and ensure compliance with regulatory requirements by utilizing smart contracts based on the blockchain. Furthermore, blockchain improves information security by giving permanent records of exchanges and touchy data.

Information Examination for Informed Independent direction: By analyzing vast amounts of data and obtaining useful insights, data analytics tools enable LLCs to make informed decisions. From monetary execution measurements to client ways of behaving, information investigation empowers entrepreneurs to distinguish patterns, expect market changes, and streamline functional proficiency. LLCs have the potential to gain a competitive advantage in their respective sectors by making use of tools like Tableau, Power BI, or Google Analytics.

Portable Applications for Far off Administration: Versatile applications have become essential apparatuses for LLC executives, permitting entrepreneurs to regulate tasks, track execution measurements, and speak with partners in a hurry. Project management platforms, expense tracking tools, and mobile banking apps all facilitate seamless remote management, allowing business owners to remain connected and productive from any location at any time.

Solutions for Cybersecurity to Protect Sensitive Data: With the rising danger of cyberattacks and information breaks, network safety has turned into a main concern for LLCs. Protecting sensitive data from unauthorized access and cyber threats is made easier by cutting-edge cybersecurity solutions like firewalls, encryption software, and intrusion detection systems. To prevent human error and ensure compliance with data protection laws, employee education programs and security awareness campaigns are also essential.

Augmented Reality (AR) and Virtual Reality (VR) for Simulation and Training: Innovative solutions for training employees and simulating real-world scenarios in LLC management are provided by virtual reality (VR) and augmented reality (AR) technologies. AR applications can provide real-time information overlays and instructions for complex tasks, whereas VR-based training programs enable employees to immerse themselves in lifelike simulations of business operations. These innovations upgrade learning maintenance and work on the productivity of preparing programs.

Enhanced Connectivity with the Internet of Things (IoT): The Web of Things (IoT) associates actual gadgets and sensors to the web, empowering LLCs to accumulate ongoing information, screen hardware execution, and computerized processes. IoT gadgets can follow stock levels, screen energy utilization, and streamline asset assignment, prompting cost reserve funds and functional efficiencies. Additionally, IoT-enabled smart devices improve workplace security and safety by instantly alerting employees to potential dangers.

Mechanical developments have reformed LLC the board via computerizing processes, upgrading correspondence, further developing security, and empowering information driven independent direction. Businesses have access to a plethora of tools to streamline operations and propel growth. These tools range from automation and artificial intelligence to blockchain, data analytics, and emerging technologies like virtual reality, augmented reality, and internet of things. As innovation keeps on advancing, LLCs should embrace advancement to remain cutthroat in the present powerful business scene. LLCs have the potential to open up brand-new opportunities for success, productivity, and efficiency by leveraging technology.

°Globalization and International LLCs

Globalization has fundamentally changed the scene of business and trade, reshaping the manner in which organizations work, contend, and team up on a worldwide scale. One of the key substances that have arisen because of globalization is the Worldwide Restricted Risk Organization (LLC), a business structure that joins components of the two associations and enterprises, offering adaptability, security, and valuable open doors for worldwide development.

Getting a handle on globalization: Globalization alludes to the rising interconnectedness and association of economies, societies, and social orders around the world. It includes the cross-border movement of people, ideas, goods, services, and information thanks to advancements in transportation, technology, and communication. Globalization has prompted the reconciliation of business sectors, the ascent of worldwide organizations (MNCs), and the rise of worldwide stockpile chains.

Development of Restricted Obligation Organizations (LLCs): Due to their adaptability, ease of use, and liability protection for owners, limited liability companies (LLCs) have grown in popularity. LLCs combine aspects of partnerships and corporations to provide owners (collectively referred to as members) with limited liability for company debts and pass-through taxation, in which members' profits and losses are reported directly on their personal tax returns.

Internationalization of LLCs: The idea of international limited liability companies (LLCs) has gained prominence as businesses attempt to take advantage of global opportunities. The operations of an international LLC are similar to those of a domestic LLC, but they involve transnational business transactions. Businesses looking to expand internationally while minimizing risks and maintaining operational flexibility will find these organizations particularly appealing.

Benefits of an International LLC:

Limited Liability: International LLCs, like domestic LLCs, provide limited liability protection for their members, shielding them from personal responsibility for the company's debts and obligations. This security is significant while working in unfamiliar words with new overall sets of laws. In terms of management structure, ownership arrangements, and operational decisions, international LLCs offer flexibility. Individuals have the opportunity to alter the organization's construction to suit the exceptional necessities of worldwide business activities.

Go Through Tax assessment: Like homegrown LLCs, global LLCs normally benefit from tax collection, where the organization's benefits and misfortunes are given to the individuals' singular expense forms. This maintains a strategic distance from the issue of twofold tax collection frequently connected with companies.

Worldwide Market Access: By laying out a global LLC, organizations get to new business sectors and potential open doors on a worldwide scale. Diversification of revenue streams and less reliance on a single economy or market are made possible by this.

Risk Mitigation: Undertaking business in foreign markets through an international LLC can help reduce the risks brought on by political and economic upheaval as well as regulatory ambiguity. The restricted risk structure shields individuals' very own resources from likely misfortunes.

Believability and Eminence: at times, directing business through a worldwide LLC can improve an organization's validity and distinction, particularly while managing global clients, accomplices, and partners.

Considerations and Challenges: Establishing and running an international LLC comes with its own set of difficulties and considerations, despite the benefits:

Legitimate and Administrative Intricacy: Working in numerous locales involves exploring complex legitimate and administrative structures, including charge regulations, corporate administration necessities, and permitting guidelines. Organizations should cautiously explore and consent to the lawful prerequisites of every nation where they work.

Cultural Differences: Understanding the cultural differences, business practices, and consumer preferences of various markets is necessary for international business. Building connections and adjusting methodologies to nearby traditions and standards is fundamental for progress.

Money Trade and Monetary Administration: Variances in cash trade rates can affect the monetary presentation of global LLCs. Compelling monetary administration and supporting procedures are important to moderate money chances and guarantee dependability.

Political and Financial Dangers: Working in unfamiliar business sectors opens organizations to political flimsiness, monetary unpredictability, and international dangers. Organizations should lead careful gamble appraisals and possibly want to relieve expected interruptions.

Obligations for Compliance and Reporting: International LLCs are required to adhere to a variety of reporting and compliance requirements in each jurisdiction in which they operate. This includes corporate governance requirements, regulatory disclosures, and tax filings, all of which can be time-consuming and costly.

Intellectual Property Protection: When expanding internationally, it is essential to safeguard IP rights. Organizations should comprehend the IP regulations and requirement components in every nation and go to fitting lengths to shield their advancements, brand names, and copyrights.

Contextual investigation: Worldwide LLC Development Consider an innovation startup situated in the US that creates programming applications for worldwide business sectors. The company decided to set up international LLCs in important markets like the UK, Germany, and Japan in order to broaden its reach and take advantage of emerging opportunities in Asia and Europe.

Statistical surveying and Procedure: The organization conducts exhaustive statistical surveying to grasp the serious scene, buyer inclinations, and administrative climate in each target market. It creates a market entry strategy that is specific to each region based on the findings.

Legitimate and Administrative Consistence: Working with nearby lawful counsels, the organization guarantees consistency with corporate regulations, charge guidelines, and authorizing prerequisites in the Assembled Realm, Germany, and Japan. It lays out auxiliary LLCs in every nation, sticking to the particular legitimate customs and documentation.

Functional Arrangement and Foundation: The organization sets up a functional framework, including workplaces, conveyance organizations, and associations with nearby merchants and specialist co-ops. It employs nearby abilities acquainted with the social subtleties and strategic approaches of each market.

Financial Management and Risk Mitigation: The company uses practices in financial management to reduce its exposure to economic fluctuations and hedge against currency risks. In order to adapt to shifting market conditions, it closely monitors political and regulatory developments and adjusts its strategies as necessary.

Licensed innovation Security: Perceiving the significance of safeguarding its IP resources, the organization documents for licenses and brand names in the Assembled Realm, Germany, and Japan. It authorizes severe privacy concurrences with workers, accomplices, and project workers to protect its restrictive innovation and proprietary advantages.

Compliance and Reporting Requirements: The business complies with local accounting standards and reporting deadlines, maintains accurate financial records, and complies with tax filing requirements in each jurisdiction. It delegates lawful and monetary counsels to direct consistency and oversee administrative dangers really.

In an undeniably interconnected world, the idea of worldwide LLCs offers organizations an essential vehicle for extending universally while overseeing gambles and expanding valuable open doors. International LLCs enable businesses to confidently navigate the complexities of international business by combining the advantages of limited liability, flexibility, and pass-through taxation.

Nonetheless, outcome in worldwide extension requires cautious preparation, steady execution, and a profound comprehension of neighborhood markets, guidelines, and social subtleties. To overcome obstacles and take advantage of the vast potential of global markets, businesses must rely on the expertise of strategic, financial, and legal advisors. International limited liability companies (LLCs) will continue to be an essential tool for businesses looking to succeed in a global economy that is becoming increasingly interconnected and competitive as a result of globalization. Companies can open up new growth opportunities and generate value for stakeholders worldwide by embracing innovation, adaptation, and collaboration.

CONCLUSION

On LLC (Limited Liability Company)

Due to their adaptability, liability protection, and tax advantages, limited liability companies (LLCs) have emerged as a popular option for real estate investors and owners of small businesses. We have looked at LLC formation, taxes, accounting, and how they are used in real estate ventures in this comprehensive analysis. By understanding the complexities of LLCs, business people can go with informed choices to upgrade their business structures and monetary techniques.

First and foremost, there are a few important steps involved in forming an LLC. Choosing a good business name, choosing a registered agent, submitting articles of organization to the state, and writing an operating agreement are all examples of these. Every one of these means assumes a significant part in laying out the legitimate system and functional rules for the LLC. One of the essential benefits of shaping an LLC is the restricted obligation security it offers to its individuals. As a result, the owners' personal assets are typically shielded from the company's debts and obligations. Because it helps reduce the risk that comes with owning property and running a small business, this protection is especially useful for investors in real estate.

Notwithstanding responsibility security, LLCs offer adaptability as far as the board design and expense treatment. Dissimilar to enterprises, which have an inflexible administration progressive system, LLCs can be overseen either by their individuals or by designated directors. Owners are able to customize the management structure to meet their specific requirements and preferences thanks to this adaptability. LLCs are regarded as pass-through entities from a tax perspective by default, which means that members report profits and losses on their personal tax returns. Because it avoids the double taxation that is associated with C corporations, pass-through taxation can result in significant tax savings for LLC owners.

However, LLCs can also choose corporate tax treatment if doing so is in line with their financial objectives. For any business, including LLCs, to be successful, it is necessary to follow sound accounting procedures. Financial reporting accuracy, tax compliance, and informed decision-making are all guaranteed by effective accounting. LLCs ought to keep up with definite records of pay, costs, resources, and liabilities, and consistently accommodate their budget reports to guarantee exactness and honesty. In the domain of land effective money management, LLCs offer a few benefits for landowners and engineers.

By holding land resources inside a LLC, financial backers can safeguard their own resources from claims and different liabilities related with property proprietorship. In addition, structuring real estate transactions through an LLC may enhance the investment's overall financial performance and provide tax advantages. With regards to charges, LLCs participating in land exercises might fit the bill for different allowances and credits, including deterioration, contract interest, local charges, and working costs.

These tax cuts can assist with balancing rental pay and lessen the general expense responsibility of the LLC and its individuals. When selling investment properties, LLCs can also use tax-deferred strategies like like-kind exchanges (1031 exchanges) to delay paying capital gains taxes. It is significant for LLCs engaged with land to keep up with legitimate bookkeeping records and comply with IRS rules to guarantee consistency with charge regulations and guidelines.

This incorporates precisely following rental pay and costs, keeping up with deterioration timetables, and documenting required tax documents, for example, Timetable E and Structure 1065. Determination, LLCs offer a flexible and powerful business structure for entrepreneurs and land financial backers the same. By giving restricted responsibility assurance, adaptable administration choices, and ideal duty treatment, LLCs engage business visionaries to seek after their business and venture objectives with certainty.

Nonetheless, it is fundamental for LLCs to execute sound bookkeeping practices and remain informed about charge regulations and guidelines to expand their monetary achievement and moderate gamble. In today's dynamic business and real estate environments, LLCs can be useful tools for building and preserving wealth with careful planning and diligent execution.

www.ingramcontent.com/pod-product-compliance
Lightning Source LLC
Chambersburg PA
CBHW052202220526
45471CB00004B/1782